BATSMAN'S PARADISE

Other books by the same author

Novels

TIMBERMILLS (1938)
THE GOLD GARLAND (1939)
COLD PASTORAL (1946)
THE HOUSE OF THE LIVING (1947)

Criticism

THE SPIRIT ABOVE THE DUST, a study of Herman Melville (1951)

WALTER HAMMOND'S COVER DRIVE
" I never saw Nijinsky, but I doubt if any gesture of his could convey the power
and the glory of motion as this superb snapshot of Walter Hammond does." (p. 110)

BATSMAN'S PARADISE

An Anatomy of Cricketomania

by

RONALD MASON

With a Preface by
E. R. T. HOLMES

" *So he turned with a passion that made up for his indolence upon Catullus, Horace, Lucretius, lying lazily dormant, yes, but regardant, noticing, with rapture, cricketers.*"

—VIRGINIA WOOLF, *The Waves.*

" *Something like this was the common undercurrent in his mind while he was reading law, or imperfectly attending to polite conversation.*"

—GEORGE ELIOT, *Daniel Deronda.*

LONDON
HOLLIS & CARTER

MADE AND PRINTED IN GREAT BRITAIN BY
THE GARDEN CITY PRESS LIMITED, LETCHWORTH, HERTFORDSHIRE
FOR HOLLIS AND CARTER LIMITED, 25 ASHLEY PLACE, LONDON, S.W.1

First published 1955

PREFACE

By E. R. T. Holmes

Ronald Mason calls *Batsman's Paradise* " an Anatomy of Cricketomania," and although I am not quite clear what he means by this, I am sure that he is right. He usually is, at any rate over his cricket facts, for having rather foolishly involved myself in an argument with him over the number of runs Jack Hobbs made in his last innings for Surrey, I found that I was wrong. There was a further slight contretemps too, when I questioned his statement about Jack Hobbs " batting all day without a cap." Jack Hobbs, I said triumphantly, invariably batted *in* a cap, but the author assured me that this was not strictly true. So did Sir John himself, when I saw him the other day and asked him this very question. My defeat was complete.

Batsman's Paradise should be a classic. It approaches the subject of cricket from an entirely new angle, and is almost as much a book on psychology as it is a cricket book, for the author has endeavoured to show how character may be profoundly influenced by an enduring passion for the game. It may take some believing, but it is apparently true that his first visit, as a schoolboy, to the Oval Pavilion some thirty years ago was directly responsible for an unnatural craving for cleanliness, which normally develops at a much later stage.

His description of the Pavilion of those days, when I had already known it for a number of years, is of particular interest to me, and although, unlike the author, I was never personally attacked by " Crackpot Number One " on the subject of the brothers Walters, I can well remember this austere individual with the piercing eye, and I can confirm the fact that he looked just like a prophet, or at least like my conception of one. This passage in particular appealed to me tremendously; while the sudden realisation, in a later chapter, that perhaps, after all, it is possible that Hammond has an aunt,

5

shows that the author, though he himself doubts if he can ever elbow his way into such company, is in fact in the Cardus/ Robertson-Glasgow class.

I do not know the author's capacity as a cricketer, but if only he could have batted as well as he writes, he would never have been out of the England side.

CONTENTS

ILLUSTRATIONS

ACKNOWLEDGMENTS

My thanks are due to Sport and General Ltd. for the frontispiece, and to Central Press Ltd. for the other photographs of first-class cricketers in this book. Those illustrating Banstead cricket and cricketers are reproduced with the friendly co-operation of my friends Messrs. B. R. Knibbs and E. Gray of the Banstead Cricket Club. Mr. B. K. Castor and the Surrey County Cricket Club I have specially to thank for the necessary permission to print the photographs of Jack Hobbs, as well as for their ready courtesy in granting me access to them and for the trouble they took to obtain reproductions for me to use.

PRELIMINARY

THIS book is the attempt of an ordinary cricket enthusiast to penetrate to a glimpse at least of the nature of the fascination which the game has for so many of his own kind. It bears the authority neither of a celebrated player nor of a professional writer on the game. It is therefore in a sense an amateur's book. I can speak from no specialist standpoint; only from the accumulated enjoyments of a spectator, player and pavilion critic experienced for more than three-quarters of a lifetime. I still play and I still watch; above all I still talk. It is partly to clarify to myself my own very varied responses to the game, but partly too to give some form to the multifarious memories of a very happy connection with it and to pass on the pleasure in a way that may help to quicken similar responses in other addicts like myself, that I have written as I have.

There are so many people to whom I feel I would have liked to dedicate this book that I am going to dispense with a personal dedication altogether. But what I would like to do is to record here and now the names of certain people whom I held very much in mind when I was writing it and whom above all others I would most like to please. All of them are prized in one way or another in my memories and reflections on cricket. Some I have played with, some I still play with; all of them I know I have talked with so constantly that I can fairly say that their presence and their conversation has built itself into that part of my life with which this book has most concern. First of all there are my father and my uncle Francis Canter, who taught me the game and watched me at it through my early youth, but who have not lived to share the subtler discussions of my maturity; and my cousin Ralph Canter who grew up with me in the idolatry of Surrey; and the friends of my remote prep-school days, John Beer and Sidney Wertheimer, and I hope they are still flourishing and retain their delighted enthusiasm; and of course Victor Buckingham, without whom this book would have had a different shape, and Duggie Dalziel, once my Greek master and now a fellow-luncher of formidable appetite, who gave me my first sight of club cricket, and well I remember it; and Denis McCartie with whom I have played and argued for years, who has been nagging at me for almost as long to write a book about cricket and now has got it, whether it is what he wanted or not; and Checks and Mike Checksfield of Banstead, who unfortunately know both a good cricketer and a good book when they see one; and Tom Evans whose cricket wit chimes exactly with my own, with whom I have played and talked until everyone else has gone home in exhaustion, so endless is the fascination that our games and our discussion engender; and the enthusiastic Leslie Johnson, half his real age in enthusiasm and keen understanding of the game, competition fiend, crossword puzzle maniac, book lover and, for his sins, Kent supporter. Then there is my wife, who, poor soul, has but little interest in cricket and quotes to me the song that Kipling wrote about the sea as the old grey widow-maker, and feels it applies even more strongly to this most non-maritime game; but she is forbearingly indulgent and helpful, although it is her belief that cricketers are sentimental adolescents and little more; and lastly my son Nick, who looks like carrying on what my father, so long ago, began. Other names, that I would also delight to honour, are celebrated, at length, in the book that follows.

There is one, however, that demands a special note on its own. To Errol Holmes, who has so generously contributed a preface to this book, I am indebted not only for that honour but for many other acts of friendly assistance. Nearly thirty years ago, when I was a hot-eyed gangling schoolboy, he and his Harlequin cap were the focus of a few years of strange and intense hero-worship on the part of myself and several friends. This culminated in one or two escapades of which I cannot even now bring myself to write, and in one egregious specimen of fan-mail, the recollection of which still sets sweat rolling down me in rivers. Even now I cannot erase the memory of that earnest schoolboy who, I suppose, exists somewhere within me still; and I think with a kind of affectionate irony of the ecstatic raptures which would have seized him had he been granted for an instant the astonishing prevision that Errol Holmes would one day write a preface to a book by his maturer self.

CHAPTER ONE

FROM RITUAL TO ROMANCE

THERE is A disconcerting profusion these days of books about cricket. The market is flooded with them in season and out; the curious fascination which draws the public to watch the game for hours, days, weeks together in the summer is transferred in the winter to every kind of printed record of its virtues and achievements. Test cricketers by the dozen write, or have written for them, their autobiographies; Test matches by the whole series are chronicled and rechronicled until the faithful reader has the scores by heart and can tell over the sequence of events in advance of the writer. (I read eleven separate books on Freddie Brown's 1950-1 tour of Australia, and for all I know there existed many more; before the spate that is following the retaining of the Ashes in 1954-5 the imagination can only flutter and retire.) On top of this, handbooks, vade-mecums, visual aids and treatises on every conceivable item from the left-hander's Chinaman and the use of the heavy roller to the degree of porousness necessary in right-hand batting gloves pour weekly from the press and are presumably absorbed by a gluttonous public always ready for more. Add to these the rare and occasional treasure of a Cardus, a Robertson-Glasgow or an Arlott enriching a worn topic with a new and individual decoration, and the idea that there can conceivably be room for a newcomer seems absurd and presumptuous indeed.

There is some justification for the general feeling that unless a writer has some contribution to make to an already overcrowded field, and unless that contribution possesses either originality or authority, he should keep off and keep silent. This is sound enough. And in the context of cricket I cannot claim authority, beyond thirty years' experience of playing it at school and club level, an experience shared by hundreds of thousands of other men; nor can

I claim anything that on the surface would suggest originality. I am just another player, average or a little below; good enough to get my school colours and play for some years in the first eleven of a reputable club; good enough to score a couple of centuries and a happy handful of seventies and eighties; good enough to catch at first slip on balance more than I drop. As spectator at first-class matches reckon me perhaps a little higher than the general, tensed by thirty years' eager and constant watching to a pitch of responsiveness that later I am going to try to analyse more closely; allow me a schoolboy's interest in the character and personality of the men playing in the middle and a maturer cricketer's analytical desire to make of every game he attends at one and the same time a drama and an intellectual exercise.

All this adds up, but not to very much. It certainly issues me no warrant to elbow in among Carduses and Robertson-Glasgows with a makeshift offering after their model. I have not even the credentials of a writer like Edmund Blunden, a modest enough performer by his own confession, but a proven poet of delicacy and perception and a sympathetic critic of the gentler imaginative levels of literature. In *Cricket Country*, a set of general meditations grouped about the central theme of cricket, Blunden illuminated his own quiet and attractive response to life without, if I may be pardoned for saying so, doing much to reveal more than a vague and drowsily pleasant conception of this game of infinite subtlety of application. The book was, beautifully and at times very movingly, about Blunden; my disappointment was the greater, and I shared it with many honest cricketers with whom I have discussed it, in that it was not very effectively about cricket. Naturally cricket was his springboard, his runway if you like, along which he journeyed into speculative flights of great charm and variety; but my enduring regret is that he launched himself, became airborne, too soon. Perhaps he kept before his eyes a saving sense of proportion, a feat difficult of achievement by the addict; he retained a grasp on relative values, cricket in his eyes taking a subordinate place to the disquisitions of wider application into which it led him.

Who am I to quarrel? I can only comment sadly enough that cricket demands to be dwelt on. That is my excuse for appearing to essay over again what a greater artist has already seemed to try; to

satisfy myself, and those honest cricketers I spoke with, that cricket
can stand up to sustained contemplation on other than statistical or
merely sensational levels, and return to the careful and sympathetic
watcher some reward more enduring than the fun of a good game
would seem to promise or warrant. To analyse, for my friends the
players and myself, some of the exquisite delights that it can so
satisfyingly provide, is the first task I would like to set myself; and
I would try to go on from there to relate this curious experience, or
set of experiences, to the wider contexts of the human imagination.

This all sounds, in the abstract, terrifyingly pretentious, and as
soggy as underdone suet pudding. If it were all to be a theoretical
analysis, the actuality would be worse than the conjecture, and we
should be choked in the smoke and smother. But cricket happily
abhors theory, having rather more of that commodity to cope with
than most games; and very little of value on this topic can communicate itself without the authenticity of personal experience
distilled through a living mind. It will be the story of the ordinary
reactions to our familiar game of an ordinary performer with
nothing to recommend him but an undying enthusiasm.

Therefore, to be authentic, the narration must be first-hand. I
shall not trouble you with the story of what Arthur Wood said to
Verity when Cameron had hit him for 30 in an over; I shall not tell
all over again, tempting as it is, the progress from crisis to crisis of
the Oval Test of 1902—what Hirst said to Rhodes, and whether he
said it at all, is not evidence. The meat of this book will be the
impact upon me of the incidents and personalities, the ritual and the
romance of such cricket as I have known during my own lifetime;
known and played, known and watched, known and followed,
known and discussed; known because responded to with the
emotions peculiar to cricket, in that restricted region of the blood
and the heart devoted to it. In this way it may become clearer why,
for example, a short and light-hearted partnership between Woolley
and Chapman one September morning at the Oval thirty years ago
has sustained me in the memory at countless incongruous moments
since, in bodily sickness or mental stress; why a particular long-past
sun-flooded May day at Hove, when Cook made 161, and the
patient Charlie Parker wheeled up over after over without result
from the sea end where I parked myself and talked of Browning to a

friendly stranger, should bring me near to tears with happiness and an association of the taste of ginger biscuits whenever I recall it; or why a particular vantage-point at the Oval, near the main score-board, where in 1921 I sat with my father, and in 1953 with my son whom he did not live to know, should bring before my mind so regularly and insistently the theme that is not far from the whole seminal purpose of this book—the theme of the continuity and the destructiveness of Time.

There has been too much moral claptrap talked and written about this game in the past for it to be possible to write objectively about it without a fairly systematic clearing out of cant. I do not accuse the reputable journalists of originating or perpetuating a stickiness that still, in this rationalist machine-age, persists, so that those who are not simple-minded enough to be hoodwinked by the spurious are (as deplorably) alienated from the genuine; but no other game that I know of has attracted to itself such a peculiar blend of sentimen-tality and homiletics, and one of its major triumphs is that its popularity and beauty have survived it. I do not now feel that the uncomfortably superheated ethical strain, injected from pulpits and schoolrooms during the last century and culminating in the embarrassing utterances of Sir Henry Newbolt, remains a very serious menace to the proper understanding of cricket. It has worked itself out, not a moment too soon; but there are grounds for suspecting that the moral superimposition has been replaced by the artistic one, and that the game is in danger of being hag-ridden by an æsthetic whimsy as crippling in the long run as all the straight bats in *Tom Brown's Schooldays* put together. For this development there are many illustrious sponsors, from Barrie to Cardus (though the latter has in a measure done public penance for his guilt), and I regard it as a far more insidious danger than its predecessor. The game itself is of a nature to attract it; in May, under blue skies against a background of laden chestnut trees and hawthorn hedges, it most scandalously courts it. The temptation is terrible, and the wily man's reaction from it (into statistics) is almost as unbearable as the original indulgence can be. Nevertheless that indulgence is to be deplored. Cricketers' whimsy is a deadly disease; and the numerous celebrated utterances of Sir James Barrie on this topic are signal crying examples of its destructiveness.

Barrie earned great fame and respect during his lifetime and after his death for his devotion to cricket and his wise animadversions on its spirit. I would not dream of questioning his devotion; but it is time that someone had the courage to record the stark fact—that his publications and pronouncements on the game are of a sentimental irrelevance that cries to the heavens. We could stand the Reverend John in *The Admirable Crichton* if we did not suspect that Barrie admired him; we can overlook the famous speech at the dinner to the 1930 Australians, a happy piece of fancy on an informal occasion; but the harlequinade of *The Allahakbarries* it is difficult to forgive. He was not playing cricket, he was playing *at* it. The dismal *facetiæ* of *The Allahakbarries* were private jokes that need not have been made public. The cricket he writes of seems a singularly pointless and joyless pursuit. No wonder he was obliged, as in his more serious work, to hide his constitutional melancholy behind a mask of dainty and inimitable jest.

Cricket has its own romance, but we must look for it elsewhere. It is a romance built on the solid foundation of its own ritual—after the manner, surely, of all genuine romance, and because of the binding relevance of that analogy we can trace its tough heredity with a genuine sense that we are not deceiving ourselves. But I do not mean to probe as yet into the nature of its romantic appeal; too much theorizing is bad for any game, most of all for this one, where the feel of the ball in the palm, the swinging balance of the bat, even the sweat under the cap peak or the mellow warmth of the midday sun across the shoulder-blades, are the core and essence of sensation from which all conjecture must start. Whatever we feel about this game must spring from certain deeply felt and long-treasured experiences, all the culmination of a moment's energy at the peak of some greater or lesser crisis. For me, such incidents are so random and various that to order them at all is an arbitrary process; certain off-drives of Woolley's played with an almost apathetic grace; a memory of the limber feline run-up and uncoiling action of Macdonald contrasted with Larwood's controlled and flailing concentration of assault; two cracking hooks of Duleepsinhji's, two whiplash square-cuts by G. T. S. Stevens—all these and the hundreds that they represent form each a tiny emotional starting point in my own progress towards a more comprehensive appreciation of this

game in its variety and richness—an appreciation which demands
the experience first and the leisurely synthesis after.

From the simplicity of the straight immediate enjoyment of an
uncomplicated incident—say one of Stevens' square cuts I men-
tioned, which were both off Tate, I may say, and were beauties,
ironically enhanced by the fact that in the next over Tate sent
Stevens' off stump cartwheeling in a glorious parabola that a
quarter of a century has not obscured—we can soon graduate to the
higher tensions of a more complex remembered moment. There
was one such in the great Oval Test of 1953, when Harvey swung
under a Trueman bouncer and the ball steepled, dragged the packed
leg-side fielders after it like a cry of hounds as it soared and dropped.
Apex of the tensed fierce arrowhead, Bailey, Laker, Lock, ran
Hutton in the certainty (if he could take time off to register awareness of it) that the whole of the 30,000 crowd and uncounted
millions at their sets ran agonizing with him. The soar and swoop
of the towering mishit not only took Hutton and his fielders with
it; it levered the greater part of that concourse out of their expensive
seats with their hearts hammering hard and their breaths held
desperately for the climax; and when Hutton, going full pelt with
his back to the batsman, lost his cap and caught the ball, the
liberating roar that shook the gasometer to its foundations comprised so much more than applause for a fine catch and relief at the
departure of a menace that it would need a book as long as the
present one fully to explain its implications.

The quick spontaneous movement in that incident, the communal
emotion born of it and linked with it, anchor it unmistakably to its
origin in ritual. All games of course conform to a recognized pattern,
and every pattern repeated has an analogy with an ordered rite; and
if we allow the acknowledged charm of cricket to reside in its
natural pattern, we can approach nearer to its essential quality by
examining that pattern than by diversion to the adventitious
trappings of morality or æsthetics. And if we approach it aright we
shall find that the æsthetic deviation was not so extreme an error
after all, for though the essence of the game is a contest the manner of
it is so patterned as to form an almost unwilled æsthetic of its own;
and while the tension resides in the contest, the charm resides in the
pattern. The balance of the two gives it depth and beauty.

"The detail of the pattern is movement"—Eliot might have been, but wasn't, considering this very topic. Leaving the contest for the moment altogether out of account, taking the detached spectator's view only of the immediate evolutions being performed in an almost routine casualness, it is impossible to overlook a considered tempo, a controlled and regulated sequence, in the seemingly haphazard comings and goings of the players on the field. It is as nearly a ballet as to make no difference; I would say that the interrelated movements on a cricket field from one end of a match to the other were highly promising subjects for a choreographer were it not that they have their own music and rhythm, and are sufficient in themselves without piling artistic glosses upon them. Like Housman's poems (and here I plunge into the thick of a heresy) they need no outside assistance, of however decorative an artistry, to express their essential beauty. No *corps de ballet*, though trained in the most exacting tradition, could have equalled the spontaneous dynamic uprising of Lindwall's congregated slip-fielders when in that same great match with his fourth ball of the first England innings he reared a scarifying bouncer at the peak of Hutton's cap and all but crowned the day with the costliest wicket of all.

Yet that moment, magnificent as it was, had too dramatic an intensity to stand as example of the basic rhythms which constitute the central charm of cricket. If this game and its incidents were continually hoisting the spectators breathlessly half out of their seats it would soon be found unnecessary to provide seats at all and the atmosphere would become superficially (and, I think also, essentially) indistinguishable from Highbury on a damp Saturday afternoon in November. The soccer crowd is a rampant participant in a restless surging turmoil of activity through which the ball threads its way, often with the assistance of a beautifully controlled and executed artistry. The cricket crowd, on the other hand, is rarely poised for the kill; it sits back on its haunches and is passive and receptive—moods which Keats for one distinguished as the truly creative. It is conditioned to this receptivity by many factors, some of which are cricket's own responsibility and some of which are not. Taking the latter first, the weather and the warmth and the surroundings have themselves enormous potency. It would be idle to deny that the ideal vision of cricket is achieved against a murmurous background of blue skies and whispering leaves, the deep cool greenness of the shadows throwing up into bright and lively relief the white figures of the players and the screens and the red spasmodic flash of the ball. (My own astringent requirements would specify blue caps, appropriately crested, for the cricketers, as I am temperamentally unsympathetic to the bright varieties commoner some years ago than they are now.) Yet it would be even idle to deny that cricket has to be played on occasions, many of them highly important ones, in surroundings and in weather which do violence to this romantic picture; it can be played as well as ever, and frequently very much better, against a drop-curtain of spattering rain whipped by a north-west wind across a vista of corrugated iron sheds and factory chimneys; the ball will be a sodden black, barely distinguishable in the brooding gloom. Yet even in these conditions cricket retains its irresistible appeal; the ritual magic extends its powerful attraction so potently that few passers-by can deny themselves the luxury of a linger and a look at just one more ball. (The plight of the train-bound passenger, who cranes desperately but never sees a ball actually bowled, is notorious and would make a study in frustration all on its own.)

It is this seminal simplicity of rhythm, expressed in its curious ritual form, that is at the heart of cricket's peculiar attraction. The tempo of the rhythm, against which all non-cricketers so persistently rail, provides the element of hypnotism necessary to the charm, like the tick of a grandfather clock in a quiet room. The warmth and the weather, when they are favourable, are powerful aids; when they are not, the charm abides on the memory of them and leaves the sympathetic imagination to supply them; but as I have insisted before, the rhythm and the ritual are independent of them. They exist in Time, and momentary variations hardly disturb them.

Consider the moving pattern; it uses to the full not only time but space. At the beginning of the movement the field is green and empty, the waiting wickets anticipating action and imparting points of significance to what otherwise would be a void. Then, just before the appointed time for starting, the pavilion bell injects an imperious warning, screws up the anticipation a few more points, builds up to the awaited first glimpse of the umpires. These come slowly and with a due dignity, knowing that it is always true that the first in a procession is never the most important but knowing too the real histrionic value of that first; and drawn on a lengthening and invisible tape behind them come first singly and then in broken active groups the fielding side, the ball flying from hand to hand, the wicket-keeper waddling stiffly in his pads and easing his cumbrous gloves; lastly, after a duly timed and dramatically most significant interval, arrive the two batsmen lonely in their championship out in the middle of the cause of their own team hidden in the pavilion's recesses. Long custom and a careful sense of propriety has timed these intervals to a nicety; they have the due discrimination of art and I would not have them changed or rushed.

These manœuvres are of course merely a prelude; but without them the significance and the suspense would be indefinably lowered. The batsman taking his guard, marking his block, hitching up his trousers, touching his cap, looking round the field; the bowler stripping off his sweater, pacing to his mark, rolling up his sleeves, flicking up the ball, giving a limbering hoist to his shoulders; the wicket-keeper jack-knifing to a menacing squat, the slips straddling to a comfortable alertness; the captain moving from the bowler's side to his place, say, at mid-off, glaring round once or twice and motioning a distant third man back against the ropes with two flicks of his fingers—all these movements lead inevitably to the culminating moment, the silent instant of tension as the bowler begins his run, the fielders in front of the wicket move off on their rhythmic lurking inward stalk, and the wicket-keeper, the slips, and above all the batsman, stiffen into a concentrated rigour that the next second will break, and break dynamically.

From that moment the pattern may resolve itself in a hundred thousand ways, predictable enough in theory, but in practice as arbitrary and enchanting as the ripples in the surface of a stream whose banks and eddies are constant but whose flurries vary infinitely from second to second. The whole wide space of grass, empty at first, is now the giant drawing board for a live tracery of movement, the white figures closing in and revolving about the red, the red sometimes (as in Hammond's cover-drive or Washbrook's hook) dashing an arrowy straight line clear through the circling satellites of fielders, and ever and again at regular intervals—note the importance of the regularity once more here—

the whole system reverses and oversets itself and the movement
defies monotony by operating from the other end. On the fringes
of the circle the movements are generous and graceful (the thirty-
forty-yard run round the boundary, the long hanging throw into
the wicket-keeper's hands); the nearer to the centre the brisker they
become, until at the heart of the movement we are down to the
constants; the bowler's leisured withdrawal and accelerating turn and
run-up, for one: and for the other, less regular but as inevitable, the
quick stitching to and fro of the batsmen as they run, each pulled up
at the wicket by his partner's opposite volition as if regulated by an
intricate pulley-and-block: this, the simplest and the most arresting
routine of the whole intricate game, is a masterpiece of spontaneous
unison in which each partner, in fulfilling his own duty, automatically helps the other to complete his too. Stitch, stitch, stitch; the
batsmen run and turn, run and turn, the ball is fired in to the
wicket-keeper, back it goes to the bowler, down gets the batsman
on his bat again, the wicket-keeper on his hunkers, the slips tensed
and avid on their toes; up comes the bowler, over goes his arm,
whip goes the ball into the gloves as the batsman covers up with his
bat in the air, flip it goes back to the bowler, the slips relax, the
batsman ambles out and prods at a spot before hitching his trousers
again and settling into his crease, the wicket-keeper takes his gloves
from the " at-ease " position behind his back, creaks again into the
" ready," and the ritual proceeds.

The detail of the pattern is movement; the recurrence of the
movement at such ordered intervals marks off time-sequences as
significant in the flexible succession of the game's diversity as beats
are in music. One ball, one over, is much like another; in isolation
the six balls bowled at the day's beginning vary hardly a jot or a
hairsbreadth from the six at the day's end; the six balls I saw
Arthur Gilligan bowl to H. L. Collins to open the Sussex *v.*
Australians match at Hove in the late August of 1921 differed no
doubt little enough in quality or intention from the six that Bedser
bowled at Hassett in 1953 at the Oval to launch the final Test on its
passage into history. Yet between the first two balls that Gilligan
loosed joyfully from the sea end (and I have them in memory still,
with Collins' sardonic shadowed face under the green mushroom
cap drily appraising them) there was as marked and as final an

interval in time as there was in the long and bedevilled generation that followed, in the thirty-two years between my first sight of the Australians and my latest. And just as two consecutive balls in one over mark off, whether for player or spectator, an interval in the inevitable progress of Time, so two overs, two innings, two matches, two seasons, accumulate on the head of the cricketer or the addict and tick off for him with an inexorable decisiveness peculiar to no other sport or occupation the passage of the years. The day's play begins in the bright fresh forenoon, voyages happily under the high sun until the luncheon hour, burns on in the hot afternoon as the wicket dusts up and the bowler's footholes deepen; takes after tea the reminiscent evening glow of the declining light, crowds to its end among grotesquely protracted shadows, and retreats into memory leaving only the torn, worn footmarks at each end of a roped space as record of a sequence that has been. Similarly the cricketer will recognize behind the unchanging rites the inevitable revolution of the seasons; the heavy candled chestnut trees of May watch over the early shivers and stiff tentative strokes in the misty light; June flowers all over the hedges and loosens the joints with hot noons and mellow bright evenings, while the hard true wickets of July, grown dusty and a little tired in August, freshen to a green St. Martin's summer in the unnatural dazzle of September afternoons that the creeping chill of the implacable autumn evening chases away at tea-time. Lunch, tea, close of play; May, June, July, August, September; season by season the patterns are renewed, and for a time the pattern-workers are renewed along with them.

The rhythms of change imposed upon patterns that are always the same; in these we can isolate for the moment the peculiarly musical charm of cricket. We have thrown the moralists overboard, we have vindicated at least in part the challenge of their rivals the æstheticians, we have, I hope, cleared our minds of some, a little, of the cant. Yet there is perhaps a danger if we leave it there; we may dehumanize it somewhat, incline to overlook that it is an elaborate interweaving, not of puppets set jangling and dancing like the figures on an old musical-box whose movements are predetermined and monotonous, but of numbers of human beings who are individuals, and sometimes characters, in their own right. It is perhaps the actuality of character and its relations with the game

that has deceived some of the more earnest among men into linking
certain reactions to the specialized crises of cricket too speciously to
the more universal crises of social, and even spiritual, life. I regret
to say that I have never known dubious morality to impair the
splendour of an off-drive or the intelligence and finesse of a long and
calculated spell of bowling to rule once and for all out of count
a mean and grasping rapacity of nature. The fallacy is fraught with
serious moral danger, and it must be suppressed. The æsthetic
fallacy (if it be one at all) trenches less on the imponderables, and
imperils no souls by the way.

But the game *is* human, and the ritual is not a ritual in a mechanical
void. I have seen this game, inside and out, ever since I can remember holding a bat the right way up as my father bowled to me on the
lawn, for more than thirty years. I have seen it from the top tier of
the Lord's pavilion and from the batsman's end of the wicket on the
3rd XI ground at Banstead, from the school team dressing-room
and from what used to be the shilling seats at the Oval, from deep
square leg in my first palpitating house match and from first slip for
a happy scratch team on the curious little ground at Jordans in
Buckinghamshire. I was once missed at silly mid-off by the Nawab
of Pataudi; what I am certain would have been a cracking four past
cover was once most brilliantly and infuriatingly cut off by D. J.
Knight. I was once hit sickeningly on the jaw by a Test match fast
bowler; I once humiliatingly ran out a very good friend and
partner by taking a quick single to the best cover point then in
England. I have been stumped by a Hampshire wicket-keeper and
caught by a Surrey one; I have caught one Cambridge Blue in the
slips and been utterly bowled by another by a ball I never saw. I
have hit an ex-Surrey captain over his head into certain tennis-
courts; a future Yorkshire batsman (when about 15 years old) was
once caught off my bowling; I have let slip a screaming straight
drive off the cricket correspondent of the *Observer* through my
hands over my shoulder into the refreshment tent. I have been
bowled at, in a nice safe net at Gamage's, by Harold Larwood;
I have spoken to Jack Hobbs. In between these bizarre high-lights
of an otherwise modest career I have scored an enormous number
of ducks and a gratifying little batch of happy little double-figure
scores, caught some satisfying catches, and enjoyed the game, the

watching, the waiting, the fetching, the carrying, the anger, the disappointment, the nerves and the occasional lovely successes, with a relish and a response that may be childish but which increase rather than diminish with the years. Into the ritual I have incorporated my own personal romance. And because no one can write about the general romance of cricket with any satisfaction to anyone else, but only of his own; and because his own is his genuine contribution to the common vitality of this game that no familiarity can seem to stale; because of this I have set out on this attempt to translate into meaning that may awaken response in fellow cricketers and others one man's secret and obscure delight in it; that by clothing the essential ritual with the flesh of one man's personal romanticism I may not only approach nearer to an answer to the æsthetic and philosophical questions that cricket always poses for me, but re-create for others in words sensations that may be as fascinating and evocative for them as they are for myself.

CHAPTER TWO

BRIEF ENCOUNTER

THE preparatory school which I attended just after the end of the First World War was housed in a tall and rambling private residence on the outskirts of Esher, one of Surrey's more ambitiously exclusive suburban towns. It stood in grounds which were approximately equally divided between bosky lawn, flourishing vegetable garden, and a playground part pavement and part gravel, where in due season a fearful free-for-all and cut-throat version of cricket was played. You had to keep the ball down (and horribly difficult it was, especially as it was a tennis ball) for if you hit it to mid-wicket over the trellis into the vegetable garden you were plumb out of bounds and you retrieved it on pain of unmentionable disciplinary action, and if you hit it over extra cover into the next-door garden a horrible old woman put her head out of a bedroom window and screamed death and destruction at you, and though hard words buttered no parsnips they returned no lost balls either. Surprisingly this breathless makeshift game was hugely enjoyable and beneficial; it sharpened the wits and quickened the eye, and I still remember with mingled surprise and pride the tingling satisfaction of my first one-handed catch.

This playground was not the whole story. Every summer afternoon in term-time we repaired in a body (we were not a large school, and there were frequently barely enough to make up the twenty-two) to the vast spaces of the local cricket club's magnificent ground. Its slope was worse than Lord's; and the young fast bowlers of eight to eleven used this menacing natural hazard with terrific abandon. I passed this ground not long ago and found that it had sadly shrunk in actuality; in my memory of 1921 it remains an illimitable space, with the pavilion reared high on the top of the slope in one corner, and a clutch of little prep-school boys strutting and squabbling away in another. It is still a fine ground; it was the inevitable background to my sleeping and waking ideas of all hard-ball cricket—in my mind's eye all grounds in the world exactly resembled it, just as the Garden of Eden was (and still is) a replica of the front garden of my earliest home. The Esher ground is unique in my recollection as the place of my cricket engendure; and I marked with a secret pleasure and pride some few years ago that the Esher club was honoured by the occasional inclusion in its team of the great Walter Hammond. I am very well content that the grass I learned my scratching cricket on should for a little time at least have been scorched by those unimaginable cover-drives.

Our headmaster was a hale scholar and sportsman, getting on in years, white-headed and a little stooped, short-tempered and irritable at times but as a general rule reliably good-humoured. He retained from somewhere or other traces of a country origin, wore tweeds and smelt of strong tobacco, and smoked a pipe in the classroom, which contrary to accepted standards lost his lessons no dignity but gave them an informal and club-like air. We ate our meals in a dark dining-room off heavy old dark-oak refectory tables; there were trophies on the mantelpiece and a vast oar along the wall, relics of the headmaster's Oxford days. (Every summer he put on his best hat and went to Henley; he was that kind of man.) He was an aloof figure and we were all afraid of him; but his aloofness did not prevent an unusual informality at table. He sat at the head of the table, his Welsh wife, many years his junior, on his left, the assistant master at the foot. (This assistant master, a curious fanatical creature with a glass eye, alternated infectious charm and enthusiasm with moods of raging ferocity.) The headmaster presided like a father among his family, carving the joint, passing the potatoes, inviting second helpings; and during the meal he would—and mark the informality intensified here—read the paper (it was the *Daily Mail*) and scatter little snippets of information out of it casually, like an off-hand husband at a breakfast table. It was in this random and familiar way that I, a goggling innocent of nine, was apprised of the first hot news of the Thompson-Bywaters murder; and in the same way and, for all I can recollect, in the same breath, was tossed among us the even more amazing information that Warwickshire had put Hampshire out for 15. (Whether he told us the staggering sequel, or whether it seemed too tall a story to tell to schoolboys, I cannot remember.)

Cricket was a part of the constant background at this school; even the crazy assistant master was an addict, and once made a century of which he was immensely proud, though as it was off the bowling of a variegated collection of nine- and ten-year-old schoolboys without benefit of coaching I doubt if its intrinsic value could be rated very highly. It was the austere headmaster himself who unbent sufficiently in Latin one day, when a boy construed " *ad dominos* " as " to lords," to reply with a chuckle, " What? To Lord's to play against Middlesex? " a sally which drew a far larger laugh than the good man was accustomed to command.

Occasionally he would even come and join in our game on the Esher ground, standing very upright and straight-batted at the wicket and running with a solemn flat-footed dignity. He bowled crafty off-breaks which I know were too much for me, and which, I took great consolation to learn, had once in some unspecified past been too much for D. J. Knight (that same D. J. Knight who was later so cruelly to cut off from a certain four my slashing cover drive). And when he did not play he would frequently watch, and when he was not watching he would go for stately walks with his young and vivacious Welsh wife, or prune his apple trees, or dig in his potato-patch, or instruct an old Boris Karloff-like gardener about his strawberry beds, or veil himself to tend his bees, or calm good-humouredly his wife's volatile excitement about the prowess of their two young sons, one of whom was about seven years old and the other, a striking *gamin* with great saucer-eyes and a heavy dark fringe, some three years younger.

There were boarders at this school, and I remember two of them well—in fact I cannot remember the others at all. The elder, Arthur Osmond by name, was a tall, slim, gentle fellow from Coventry, with manners beyond his age and a free style in batsman-ship. An enthusiastic Warwickshire supporter, he carried on the cricketing tradition of the school by possessing a father who used to write contentious statistical letters to the *Cricketer* about averages, and points per win on first innings, and matters of kindred impor-tance. The younger was an intensely vital and grotesque little Jew from Bradford, named Sidney Wertheimer, who through the juxtaposition of his initial and surname was invariably known as Squirt. His pugnacity and ebullience awakened all the detestable anti-Semitism latent in the assistant master aforesaid, who took unpardonable liberties with the unhappy boy's race and appearance (which was against him). To our undying shame we hideous little sycophants laughed; to his enduring credit the indomitable Squirt shouted back. He fought tooth and nail for his dignity and his creed, this vivid little Jew-boy from Bradford; he endured humiliation after humiliation at the hands of this bully (who, God help him, did I think no lasting harm and to do him justice did not maltreat the boy physically); and I have often wished to meet him again and do a little reparation for some of our infant caddishness. But Squirt hung on, his humour and vitality unimpaired; and when he left I lost sight of one of the most resilient and attractive characters I have ever known. What possessed his Bradford parents to send him to this ordinary little prep school 200 miles from home I could not guess; but they sent to London and to exile one of the most perfervid Yorkshire cricket supporters it has ever been my fortune to meet. He was not very good at the game himself; he was, as my mother used to say, " all legs and wings," and he ran like a dromedary and caught like a girl; but he was steel-keen. Wilfred Rhodes and Emmott Robinson had no more fanatical advocate, and in their time they had plenty. We were assailed at all appropriate and inappropriate hours with the virtues of Holmes, Sutcliffe, Rhodes, Oldroyd, Robinson, Dolphin and Macaulay, the Kilners and the Wilsons (this was the great heyday of Yorkshire cricket and we were not allowed to forget it); so untiring was his advocacy that when one day the paper announced the untimely death of the Lancashire fast-medium bowler James Tyldesley, and the assistant master in one of his less *farouche* moments of jocularity kidded the impressionable Squirt that it was Rhodes who had died, his immediate and crushing dismay was so genuine that although we were by now very ready to be sick at the name or sight of a Yorkshireman we had not the heart to keep up the pretence. Squirt it was, too, who in the geometry lesson conducted (not without severe cerebration) by the headmaster, who was a Classics man, took advantage of a quiet moment while the Head stood contemplating a problem on the blackboard with his back to the class in an evident throe of mental perplexity to exclaim in a hoarse and reverberating stage whisper " Stumped! " and thereat elevated his forefinger like an umpire; awakening from the trance of extreme delight and self-satisfaction consequent upon his own merry conceit to find himself facing a silent withering glare from the old man himself, who had turned with a noiseless dignity to see what was going on.

Osmond left before my last summer term at this school, and so did John Beer, another close cricketing friend of mine, with whom I shared the long walk home. This Beer was mightily knowledge-able about the first-class game, was the first person to show me a copy of *Wisden*, and enlivened our trails to and from school with an enormous amount of variegated information about cricket and cricketers, accurate and otherwise, that I think has been the founda-tion of the vast and shapeless structure of indiscriminate learning about the game with which I have encumbered my memory since. He had a dream one night in which he read a momentous score-sheet starting " Hobbs 130, Russell not out 588," and the rest of his career while I knew him seemed bedevilled by the anticipation of this vision coming true. However, he left before the desired consummation, and his young brother who remained did not share his passion for cricket; so with John Beer and Osmond gone, the fanaticism remained, for my last summer term, chiefly in the hands of Squirt and myself.

The boarders, being few, lived almost like members of the headmaster's family. From limited scraps of conversation at the dinner table it appeared that they shared family meals, family gossip and for all I knew the family hearthrug. With this in mind I was both surprised and not surprised to hear Squirt announce to the table generally one lunch-time, in comment apparently on some remark of the headmaster's that I had missed, " I see he made firty-seven yesterday " (Squirt's mouth was, as usual, full, and he had a congenital inability to pronounce his th's).

Now something suddenly clicked in my mind—I read the scores even more avidly and attentively than Squirt—and I tumbled to the exciting fact that a new arrival in one of the provincial counties, who had attracted my attention because he carried the same surname as the headmaster (and who had, as Squirt said, made 37 the day before), was apparently connected to the headmaster more closely even than in name. It came out then that he was his nephew; and from that moment I followed this newcomer's progress with an avuncular benevolence. He was playing, as it happened, for Warwickshire; and the buzzing excitement, that this unexpected link with immortality had around the lunch table and in the school generally, mounted to a tingling flurry of expectation when we realized a week or two later that Warwickshire were due in a few days' time to present themselves, like my schoolfellow's ambassadors, *ad dominos*, at Lord's, to play against Middlesex.

At this, unheard-of mutterings and whisperings took place in and around the corridors and form-rooms. We were all to have a holiday; we were all to be taken to Lord's; a selected few were to be taken to Lord's; the family *only* were to go to Lord's; none of us, not even the family, were to go to Lord's. High anticipation was running like electrified wire around our little closed circle; and when the omens proved unfavourable an elaborate round-robin, I seem to remember, was drawn up for presentation to the headmaster, beseeching him of his bounty to let us all accompany him on this auspicious family occasion. At this interval of time I cannot remember whether this petition ever got presented; if it did, it was unsuccessful. The arrangements leaked out; the family, the headmaster and his wife and their elder boy, would go on Wednesday, the first day. The rest of us (and Heaven knows, there was no good reason why we should ever have thought of doing otherwise) would stay at school and get on with our work.

We naturally fumed with anger and disappointment, and a lot of cheap cracks were levelled at the favouritism bestowed on the headmaster's son, who couldn't even play the game respectably, much less understand the finer points as displayed by his cousin Bob and the others at Lord's. However, nothing could be done about it, and sure enough on Wednesday morning off went the family in high feather, the headmaster wearing his best Henley hat, leaving the assistant master, who would probably have liked to go too, to cope with a collection of disgruntled schoolboys with more than half a hope that it would rain and spoil their day.

Well, it didn't rain, and we read in the evening papers that the headmaster's nephew had made only 5, so we philosophically reconciled ourselves to the disappointment and felt that hard as it was on the cricketer, it had served the family right. Nevertheless, these eminently Christian sentiments were whistled bravely down the wind when I got to school next morning to help crow over the headmaster's son and was met with the breathless information that the great man himself, the headmaster's nephew Bob in person, had been staying the night in that very house, was indeed in the form-room at that very mortal minute, and would presumably, at a pinch or at a price, it was not clear which, offer to the humblest character present the hem of his garment to be touched.

The fearful fracas in the form-room resolved itself into Squirt, fussing round the hero like a heavyweight's manager round his principal; he appeared to be acting in the self-imposed rôle of publicity agent and general factotum, warning off the importunate with a proprietary air of *noli me tangere* and welcoming the privileged to a place in the queue. The central exhibit, wondering no doubt what kind of an anteroom to Hell he had allowed himself to be cajoled into, stood modestly with his back to the fireplace, a dark stocky youth with a brooding look, mechanically turning over the pages of the *Cricketer*, presumably to retain some tangible handhold on reality. Before I came out of the trance that instantly enveloped me, I heard myself being fulsomely introduced by Squirt as (I think and believe) " *Mr.* Mason—an enfusiastic cricketer."

Enfusiastic I was and enfusiastic I remain, but the occasion called for far more than enfusiasm. I held out a quivering hand and it was graciously enveloped and returned to me. I suppose I said something; it is possible that the hero of the hour said something too. I simply cannot recall anything but a horrible feeling of looking a fool before a perfectly ordinary and unassuming young man who had done nothing to deserve either hero-worship or the semblance of it. Around us Squirt jumped and fluttered, waiting impatiently for the next presentation. The scene dissolved in mist and the bell for prayers dispelled it. I can remember only one quietly decorous remark of the central figure, delivered passionlessly in a detached reverie, " I knocked Hill's middle stump out of the ground." (He did, too, and it is still in *Wisden* for all to see.) With that the vision fades; only a kind of after-vision remains; of the headmaster's wife putting her head round the door during first lesson to say " Bob's just going," and the headmaster going out for a minute to wish him luck and say goodbye. A little later, as we struggled with our Latin sentences, we heard a car drive off, and in our hearts we wished him luck too.

He drove off that day to make his first fifty in county cricket. Within three years he was playing for the Gentlemen at Lord's. Within seven he was captaining England. The name is R. E. S. Wyatt. (The headmaster's name was Harvey Wyatt, a name I have respected and remembered with what is I hope not a presumptuous affection all my life; and the name of the fierce *gamin* with the saucer eyes and the bang of thick dark hair is Woodrow Wyatt, sometime literary journalist, socialist, Member of Parliament, and Under-Secretary for War in the Attlee administration; who has expressed in his autobiography a politely phrased exasperation that wherever he travels about the world it is R. E. S. Wyatt and not Woodrow whom people show the keenest interest in.) R. E. S. Wyatt is now a familiar part of between-war cricket history, and there have been plenty of postwar occasions when the well-known pugnacious figure has deployed that curious mixture of hedgehog doggedness and free stroke-play with nearly all his old mobility and effectiveness. The man I shook hands with in an awed trance has taken all over the world his characteristic glowering concentration, has broken in the service of his game nearly every bone in his body, some of them several times over; has batted, bowled, fielded, captained and selected at the very highest levels; and is now by way of being, while still on nodding terms with youth and energy, an elder statesman of the game. Because of that trivial encounter thirty and more years ago, I have had for the rest of my life a curious interest in his performances; and at this distance of time and disparity of accomplishment it has ceased to matter to me very much that, since that day when he shook hands kindly and then drove away to his first taste of a success that by any standards has been conspicuous, he has doubtless been surrounded very properly by so many good cricketers that he has no reason to remember that solitary ten-year-old enfusiastic one who goggled at him dumbly and was too tongue-tied to wish him well.

Much later that summer I went to see him play for Warwickshire at Hove against Sussex. Sussex batted all the time I was watching and he bowled a good deal and fielded a trifle pensively at deep third man. From hints he has let fall in his autobiography it is excusable to think that it was about this time that he was beginning to feel puzzled at the attitude of his captain, who so far from recognizing a future England No. 1 was concentrating on his comparatively innocuous medium-paced bowling and putting him in as late as No. 9. As this Sussex game ended he caught up his sweater and made speed for the pavilion with the Hove crowd descending in their friendly way upon the retreating players; I with my autograph book followed, urged by my parents to renew that momentary acquaintance and carry away tangible spoils. But at the last moment I hesitated, and I think deliberately forbore. He would not remember me, why should he? And if he didn't remember me, I didn't want his autograph. So I hung back, and he vanished; and I returned to my upbraiding parents.

I think it was 1929 before I saw him close to again. By this time I had attained the dignity of a schoolboy membership ticket at the Oval, of which much more, oh infinitely much more, later; and he was captaining a rather depleted Rest of England side against Notts, the champion county. On the first day of this match I came face to face with him in the long room in the pavilion; I a leggy and self-conscious sixteen, he in full flannels and (would it be?) an England overseas blazer. Naturally he did not know me from Adam; I, prepared for this, took a detached and pleasurable interest in observing him, momentarily, as he passed. He was matured and unbelievably sunburned; his face was leaner, had command of itself, had acquired resolution. I watched him pass on with a lingering sensation of pleased ownership. Later in the day he made over 80, batting in a style I was quick to approve. I saw him again as he left the ground in the evening, master of his fate, contented, with a straggle of urchins at his heels clamouring for his autograph. As he fled into a taxi, half a dozen books were thrust into his face; with a genial but uncompromising smile he tossed them unconcernedly out of the window. The taxi moved off spilling boys and books. Assuredly I had done wisely in not approaching him at Hove.

Late in the next season he became the centre of a sensation. Percy Chapman had deposed Carr in 1926 for the fifth and final Test at the Oval and with the assistance of one of the most powerful teams that have ever represented England had crushed Australia in a Test match of classic quality. In 1928-9 his cheerful and adventurous nature had piloted a triumphant touring side across Australia to even more comprehensive victories, owed not only to his personal inspiration but to the aggressive Tate and the pertinacious White, and to a consistency of batting that was prodigious, led by Hammond at the peak of his blazing genius. But when Australia came again in 1930 they counter-attacked with the most formidable batsman in history: Tate, Larwood, Robins, Peebles, none were of much avail, and on our side Hobbs was something less than consistent and Hammond had lost for a time the high flair. After one victory our grip slackened; a gorgeous slap-happy hundred from Chapman himself only postponed, could not avoid, a smashing defeat at Lord's; and by the time the fifth Test arrived it seemed to the selectors that a repetition of the magic recipe was the last desperate and necessary measure. Rightly or wrongly they put their trust in mumbo-jumbo; and Chapman, cheerful and unlucky, came out by that same door wherein he went. Through no fault of his own the surprised Wyatt was suddenly jerked into the centre of the limelight, and to the accompaniment of howls of public execration found himself endowed with Chapman's job and Chapman's insuperable worries.

The Press went grandly to town on it; to read some of the less responsible sheets was almost to be persuaded that Wyatt had got the job by some dishonourable and even unmentionable means. His life for the week or so that preceded this his first Test match in England, his first Test match against Australia, was made nightmarish by reporters and gossip-writers of every shade and degree of competence and integrity. Journalists attended his down-sittings and his uprisings; he was joked about on the radio (" All Wyatt on the Western Front "); anonymous letters invaded his breakfast table (one is said to have threatened assassination if he dared to show his face at the Oval on Saturday). When Saturday dawned fine and bright, I took time off from my natural preoccupation with the necessity of winning the toss and making over 400 to wonder for a minute or two how my fleeting acquaintance of seven years ago was facing his breakfast, if he could burrow down to it through the distracting heaps of threatening letters; whether on this crowning day of his life he could swallow a morsel, as he contemplated with that grimness that we all got to recognize as part of his nature the alternative prospects of immediate assassination or the captaincy of England in this Test match. It occurred to me that it would be interesting to know which of these alternatives, on that fine morning, he would have been inclined to prefer.

He escaped assassination, he won the toss, England settled down and made over 400. That on that cast-iron wicket, with the rest of the year to play with, Australia's batting steamrollered the life out of England's attack, and then caught us on a worn wet wicket at the fag-end of the week, could not be laid to Wyatt's account. He was no Chapman, he was no miracle-maker, his team had not the controlled and compact genius of the Oval team of 1926, and Australia had Bradman in his ruthless pride. Wyatt could not produce the rabbit out of the hat; I doubt if anyone expected him to. But on the first day of that furnace-like ordeal he faced his necessary conflict, perhaps the most momentous he had yet dared or was ever to dare. I expect he will remember that Saturday as long as he lives; and I who was there (I saw every single ball of that game) will remember it too, for there still lingered about my recollection of that momentary relationship the enduring sense that I had some infinitesimal right of pessession in this cricketer, that I stood in ever so small a degree *in loco parentis*. Of his agony on that day, and I am sure it must have been agony, however pleasant it may be to him in retrospect, I, sitting high on the pavilion under the clock, was a keen and sympathetic partaker. I do not suppose that he felt any alleviation for that; but if in some miraculous way he did, he could put it down as legitimate reward for the pains of that much smaller agony he had endured seven years before in the form-room at Esher.

For the gods, heaping anticipatory horrors on him all the week, did not spare him certain actualities on the day itself. A captain carries a double load; a personal and a collective responsibility. His batsmen's failures cannot be his fault, but they can add mountainously to his troubles. On a plumb Oval wicket under glorious unflurried skies, Wyatt's batsmen on this Saturday did him somehow less than justice. Wall and Fairfax were accurate and hostile, but not deadly; the most penetrating menace was provided by the formidable Grimmett, compensating doubly by superb length and flight for the dangers of the spin the pitch denied him. The accuracy and the high-pressure atmosphere together fretted the concentration of our leading batsmen; ominously the day began with a severe fright when in the very first over Hobbs and Sutcliffe were discovered at the same end, shouting at each other. Most fortunately somebody was late with the return, and Sutcliffe got back safely; but it was twenty minutes before I drew a full breath again. As it was, Hobbs and Sutcliffe played elegantly and safely enough until just on lunch-time, when Hobbs, after a cracking hook for four off Wall, repeated the stroke off the next ball and was grandly caught at square-leg by Alan Kippax. After lunch there was an evanescent 50 by Duleepsinhji, a sweet Saturday afternoon innings devoid of stamina which terminated with a spoon stroke of reprehensible casualness as if the batsman were anxious to give someone else a knock; but apart from the perennial bedrock stability of Sutcliffe the batting throughout seemed of an airy and indeterminate quality without backbone or solidity. Whysall made a few free shots off his legs which remain in the memory, Hammond achieved one incandescent slash behind coverpoint to which not a fielder moved, and Leyland for once failed altogether to move into his usual position of anchor-man. And with Leyland out just on tea-time, and the scoreboard showing 189 for five, an apathetic depression seemed to have stifled the life out of one of the strongest batting sides that England could muster between the two wars.

It was then Wyatt's turn to bat. He would not have been human if he had not been nervous; taking into account the accumulation of psychological strain to which he had been subjected during the past week, he could have been excused for being paralysed. In addition to this there were on his mind, I take it, the innumerable administrative responsibilities which inevitably attend the captaincy of an international side in a Test match, many of them altogether unconnected with the game itself; and now came the fearful moment when he was required to put to the test his skill, not only of character and captaincy, but of sheer naked batsmanship. He was the last accredited batsman in the order; there was George Duckworth to come, there were Tate, Larwood, Peebles, excellent good neighbours i' faith and very good bowlers, but as batsmen, alas, a little o'erparted. Only he and the comforting Sutcliffe stood between life and (in a measure) death. And Grimmett, full of success and guile, was to finish the over to him from the pavilion end.

How much of this crowded through his mind as he picked up his batting gloves in the dressing-room is of course nobody's business. There may have been present also a kind of sapping suspicion that he was in fact as inadequate as some of his more brutal critics and anonymous correspondents had so boldly asserted. It is quite likely that at this moment he believed he was, and that the crowd outside would be (and not secretly) not sorry if he showed himself up. He had had, after all, an insufficiency of experience at this level; and quite certainly an insufficiency of public encouragement. I doubt whether he took this public aspect of his complex problem into serious account at this instant, being quite possibly more rationally engaged in asking Leyland how easy it was to spot Grimmett's googly; but it may have contributed unconsciously or otherwise to what cannot have avoided being the father and mother of a concentrated qualm. I do not doubt that one part of him wished it were bedtime and all well; very probably another and even more vociferous part of him wished he were dead. If any man at the Oval that day had a right to feel worried, it was R. E. S. Wyatt at that moment, going out to face Grimmett for the last tense over before tea in his first Test match in England. He need not have worried.

As he appeared at the top of the pavilion steps the entire Oval rose at him like a tidal wave. I have heard applause, even frenzied and unbridled applause, on many occasions before and since. On Bradman's last appearance at the Oval nearly twenty years after this time the ovation reached proportions as impressive and as moving; but I do not think it beat it for effect. The entire Oval gave out to Wyatt, with good measure running over, the public encouragement and friendliness that its good representatives the journalists had so conspicuously failed to deliver when there was most need for it. We had heard applause before that very day; the roar that greeted Hobbs and Sutcliffe, the cheers for Duleepsinhji's 50, the very special welcome a Test crowd always reserved for Hammond. They were swallowed up in this one like odd buckets of water slung into Niagara. Every man, woman and child on the ground beat their hands together till they were sore; they roared a welcome from deeply outraged throats, they waved handkerchiefs, they drummed with their feet, they whistled. If they had possessed motor-horns or steam whistles or ship's sirens they would have given him the whole screaming works. The noise beat up against the eardrums like a storm at sea; it rolled round the vast ground in perceptible waves; as Wyatt reached the wicket at the Vauxhall end great banks of sound came volleying from the far side, volleying inexorably, answering and counter-answering the rise and fall of the great volumes of sound from the place where he had first appeared. The noise continued, thudding and insistent, even while he took guard. Only as Grimmett moved back to the end of his four- or five-yard run, and Wyatt prepared to face his first ball in a Test against Australia, did the volume decrease and die away, reverberating round the ring like the echoes of a vast explosion. As the pigeons wheeled scared and scattered to the height of the pavilion roof, I found myself (with the rest) on my feet. If anyone had spoken to me I would have cried like a baby.

How Wyatt got through that last horrifying over before tea is part of his story, not of mine. He has told it in his autobiography; he remembers it in horrible detail as one of the most harrowing experiences of his life. I merely remember it in general as a corollary to that central moment when Wyatt got his public recognition, when the Wyatt who was my private possession became for his due season and career the property of the public. As he walked out to that phenomenal reception (before which he appeared, as always, as impassive as a statue) I accompanied him both as applauder and applaudee. I was the crowd; by virtue of that huddled and trance-like moment in the classroom, I felt near enough to him to be Wyatt, in part, as well. I could have wished that Squirt could have been at my side to demonstrate, as he would certainly have done with the utmost vigour and displacement of air. Perhaps he was there, at the Oval, who knows? I hope he was. I have not seen him or heard of him since we were boys of eleven, but in the public figure of R. E. S. Wyatt our private enfusiasms have survived. I would like to think that he too remembers without regret the infantile pleasures that maturity has sustained and not despised.

Wyatt stayed in that day, after that hair-raising survival, and together with Sutcliffe welded a backbone into the England innings. When stumps were drawn he was 39 not out, and on the Monday

he carried his score to 64. Sutcliffe built up one of his monumental
centuries, and the side achieved an impressive 400 after all. Of the
systematic butchery to which the bowling was then submitted, of
the regrettable decline of the match into a massacre, we all know
enough. Sufficient for me that Wyatt had fledged himself once and
for all out of my patronage into something wider and larger—a
victory he knew nothing about. I have followed him with interest
since, of course, but with the interest I kept for Sutcliffe, Tate, any
old cricketers you like to mention. He had graduated from my
private patch into a place in cricket history.

I did not often see him bat, and it is characteristic of the secondary
place that he took thereafter in my imagination that my most vivid
memory of his after-career is of an incident in which he was
certainly the central figure but in which he somehow takes second
place. In the closing few overs of the first day of a Gents v. Players
match at Lord's, dignified incidentally by the strongest Players side
I have ever known, the Gentlemen began their innings in a fading
light in the last nerve-racking minutes, facing Larwood and Tate.
Wyatt was one of the opening pair, and his partner was A. G.
Hazlerigg, the Cambridge captain of that year, who must have felt
glad, as he peered down the pitch into the shadow of the glooming
pavilion, to have an England captain at the other end to farm the
ferocious attack and guard him from the cutting edge of these epic
opening bowlers. Yet surprisingly it was Wyatt who did not
survive. After a confident opening against the fastest England had
to offer, Tate's spitting outswinger got a touch at the outside edge.
The red snick streaked knee-high past the stood-back wicket-
keeper; third man began a despairing gallop, the ball would be at
the screen already. He could have spared his galvanic jerk;
Hammond at first slip had taken it left-handed, white-hot and
whistling as it flew, as if he had meditatively selected it, after some
thought, from a number displayed for his choice. In my memory
of that lightning incident, Wyatt has to give place to one whom he
would join with me in acknowledging as a greater.

Heartily know,
When half-gods go,
The gods arrive.

I would not dream of using Emerson's words as a stick to beat my childhood's hero with; I mean merely to measure the quality of my adherence to two sturdy and memorable characters. Wyatt, through chance entirely, was my earliest youth's closest link with big cricket; how tenuous a link this narrative will have made perfectly clear. Hammond, as I shall show later, is something quite other. Wyatt has served for me now as a beginning, an indication of how the timeless ritual of cricket began in my early days to be filled out with flesh and blood, given organic life, romanticized a little, adapted to common sentiments and emotions, given humour and intelligence. My curious relationship (quite one-sided of course) with this distinguished cricketer is an important step in the development of this beautiful game, and my response to it, from the simplicity of the rite that I set out in my first chapter to the complexity of the reality that I hope to reach in my last. If by any chance he should ever read this account of my unwarrantable use of his name and personality, I know that he, an enfusiastic cricketer if ever there was one, will recognize and perhaps have the charity to salute the genuineness of an experience which, for all I know, may once have been his own.

One regret remains: that in the pavilion at the Oval, I cannot remember whether it was at the Champion County match I told of, or at the critical Test of Wyatt's triumph, I caught a glimpse of his uncle, my old headmaster. The encounter was momentary, was over in a second, and I do not think he recognized me. Whichever day it was it must have been for the old man a day of great pride. I wish very much that I had had the wit to accost him with a word of acknowledgment, congratulation, something to show that I shared it. I think he would have appreciated it. But I was only sixteen or seventeen, gangling and unsure of myself, and I retreated, as I so often did, to an ultimate regret, as I so often do. The old man died two or three years later, and now I alone recall (for I doubt if the central figure does) the occasion that helped to develop and civilize for me one of the ruling imaginative passions of my life.

CHAPTER THREE

BOY ETERNAL

Two lads that thought there was no more behind
But such a day to-morrow as to-day
And to be boy eternal.

IT is doubtful whether it is humanly possible for a grown man ever
to play a game with the absorbed single-mindedness of a child.
I cannot speak for the professional games-player, as I have known
none well enough to open my mind to him or to get him to open
his mind to me on this topic; but I cannot envisage, even in the
keenest and most energetic of players, the continuance of that
obsessed concentration on the game, to the absolute exclusion of all
other considerations whatever, that is the prerogative of the growing
boy before he is aware of the closing of the inevitable shades. It is a
matter of social ethics whether or not this is a good thing; it would
perhaps be possible to doubt the value to society of large numbers of
young men who played games with the whole of their waking
thoughts and senses. Sir Osbert Sitwell has made somewhere a
characteristically disparaging reference to boys who excel in cricket
at school, declaring that when they take their place in adult life they
are fit for nothing but playing cricket, and he can think of no more
infantile occupation for a grown man. Within certain clearly
defined limits one can see his point. Even I, sitting at ease on the
great concrete stand behind the bowler opposite the Lord's pavilion,
have been visited from time to time with just such a heretical
thought. In the bright smiling summer afternoon a man in the
fullest flush of his youth runs certain yards and propels a ball with
great seriousness towards another man in the fullest flush of his
youth, who with equal gravity moves a pace or two on carefully
positioned feet and swings an oiled and seasoned blade of wood at
the ball as it arrives at him. In due time he and his fellow run

42

solemnly up and down (or do not), and the process is free to begin again. And the insidious thought will often surprise me, even as I joy in the ordered grace of the scene, that this bowler and these batsmen are most probably devoting not only that summer day but that whole summer, and indeed the complete economy and organization of their entire lives, to the minutest detail of just this very activity, and to this alone. These grown men (may I be forgiven) are spending their rich maturity with nothing more than a set of toys. Suppose (I say to myself in a hideous instant of what is either vision or blindness), suppose a man should elect to swing to and fro all his life in a swing such as you see in children's recreation grounds, or to attain unheard-of proficiency in wielding a skipping-rope. Would there be (this is horrible, but it has to be faced), would there be all that difference? I do not answer this question directly here, since it is a question that a lifetime of sophistry will fail either to confute or satisfy, but I pose it since it has often seemed to me that at the backs of the minds of all adults who have given themselves in whole or in part to the fascination of cricket there must linger as faintly as a barely traceable perfume this little devil of a doubt that disrupts single-mindedness. There is no doubt that these cricketers are doing less harm, far less harm, than some ostensibly more rationally employed citizens are permitted to wreak upon society with no questions asked; while they are batting and bowling they are not buying and selling shares or manufacturing armaments or editing sensational newspapers or circulating children's comics; but they are in a certain way less relevant to society, or apparently so, than the share-pusher or the sensational journalist. I believe that the irrelevance is only superficial and that is why I have written this book; and I do not believe in any case that this kind of relevance is all. But the wonder at the apparent single-mindedness of these excellent husbands and fathers making a profession, and an earnest and energetic one, out of a toy or two picked up in the back garden—that wonder remains.

Let it remain; we have to be reconciled to it. We must put it to sleep with the assurance that were it not for such single-mindedness on the part of a few, the many wearier and less fortunate who take their ease on the balconies of Lord's and elsewhere would have less of a feast of skill and emulation served up for their delight. No doubt these heresies present themselves once in a way even to the best and greatest of our favourite exponents; Bedser, as he walks back polishing the ball on his thigh, may ask himself, or his brother at mid-off, " What am I, a grown, powerful, intelligent man in the thirties, doing here? "; Compton, standing in the gully with his much-advertised hair blown back and forth about his face in the breeze, may wonder " Was it for this the clay grew tall? " That they compress these bogies of distraction to nothing is the game's gain and ours; and one of the surest reasons why they can do it is the survival in these men, the entirely attractive and fruitful survival, of those qualities in the child and the boy, of grave absorption in the moment, which so often the grown man is quick to discard unless there's money in it. (That there's money in it for Bedser and Compton they themselves would be the first to acknowledge; but I will affirm under torture that that is a very secondary, not a primary cause of this absorption.) I have no doubt at all that as Hutton looks round the field preparatory to facing, let us say, Moss of Middlesex, or as Evans, patting his gloves comfortable, goes briskly back as Ridgway takes the new ball, either or both may be assailed by the momentary thought of the income tax, or the gas bill, or the mortgage instalment, or the car repairs, or the children's measles or the school report or the wife's birthday present. They will doubtless be well enough disciplined to segregate such considerations for as long as practicable, but there can be no doubt that these considerations are there, hedging them in; and they are considerations common to mortal men and there would be no particular merit in being exempt from them. But the point I am trying to make is that the young boy bowling his guts out at school, with the intense application to the job of which few beside a young boy are capable, is untrammelled either by the philosophic worries I have arbitrarily imputed to Bedser and Compton, and, lucky man, is free even of the more mundane frettings that I have for the purposes of my argument brought home to Hutton and Evans. As he bowls, the universe around him ceases to have material relevance. He bowls because his body is for the instant geared magnificently for that purpose and for none other. He has no income-tax responsibilities or wife to buy presents for. He may have school examination and report worries, but I have met few boys addicted to cricket who let their cricket be seriously impaired by them.

I myself remember vividly in many details the four crucial years of my school life: 1928, 1929, 1930, 1931. In 1928 I took Matric. with honours, in 1929 I failed Higher Schools Certificate, in 1930 I passed Higher Schools and Inter Arts and in 1931 I collected a handful of minor prizes and scholarships and passed high in a competitive examination into the Civil Service. Yet I remember those years, emotionally, entirely differently; 1928 is for me the year when I failed entirely to find my batting form in the school 2nd XI; 1929 a year of great excitement and tension when I played with mounting success in the 1st XI but failed (I think now, unfairly) to get my colours; 1930 a year of disappointing failure to ram home the advantage, a year when I got my colours as a kind of consolation at the end of a lean season; and 1931 a halcyon glory of (for me) ease and success as an established member of the Eleven. The rise and fall of tension over those four years is vivid with me still; but it does not relate in any way whatever to the important examinations that during that same period I took, and failed, and passed.

This entirely appropriate concentration on the moment cannot wholly last into mature life; but unless a little of it endures there is no point in playing the game at all. Unless the boy can prolong himself within the organism of the man, achieve, to speak paradoxically, a kind of temporary immortality there, then a crabbed middle-aged detachment will wither first the player and then the game itself. It is not a game from which a man can disengage himself with impunity. By taking this precept too literally, many have retarded their own proper intellectual and perhaps imaginative development and called down upon their heads, in the context I have already quoted, the contempt of Sir Osbert Sitwell, and who is to say that they have not perhaps deserved it? There are assumptions and values that relate superficially to the game and that in a facile way can relate also to a wider life outside it. Hence the straight-bat heresy, from which with a blush retire.

But the pure unspoilt ingenuous keenness of youth, how sweet it would be to recover it! With what avidity I plunged into the highly organized routine cricket in the junior half of my public school, which was King's College School, Wimbledon, where in two afternoons every week in the games considered more promising (and in the succession that culminated in " Major," the game from which the Junior School First XI was chosen) lots of little correctly dressed automata were turned out off the assembly belt to a preordained pattern, gifted with a patent left-foot-forward, nose-over-the-ball push which sent every ball with the utmost elegance and correctness a few feet short of a not very deep cover-point. From the slightly eccentric and individualistic atmosphere of my prep school, with its extravagant assistant master, its tenuous connections with R. E. S. Wyatt, and its tenure of the Esher cricket ground, I dived with intense adaptability, almost hysterical, into the decorous orthodoxy of this elaborate organization for the manufac-ture of correct cricketers. So eager was I to sample this new element that I was half-way to the wicket to begin my first innings, brim-ming over with confidence and anticipatory delight, when I had forcibly to be dragged back to remove my blazer, which in the excitement I had forgotten to take off. I accepted the solecism at its context value, was overwhelmed with confusion, and count myself fortunate that it did not ruin my self-control. I made enough runs in this game, a lowish one into which I had been drafted under the quite legitimate impression that my cricket would be as deplorable as my football, to win promotion to the next highest (" Minimus "), considered a breeding-ground for future prospects for ultimate honours; and here in my first game I went in at the fall of the fourth wicket to join a vigorous and optimistic cricketer by the name of Victor Buckingham, already marked down in official circles as a player of considerable promise and infinite keenness.

The stand that followed, if it could be reckoned by intensity of excitement and potentiality value, remains in the memory as something altogether out of the ordinary, measurable in runs to the total of shall we say 120 or so. (You must remember how old we were at the time; I was eleven and he was ten.) My sober and statistical recollection is bound to record two undoubted certainties: *one*, that by the rules of every game except " Major," where the limit was 25, you were obliged to retire at 20; and *two*, that I quite distinctly remember being bowled for 12. It is difficult to see, therefore, how our stand could with any degree of probability have exceeded 30; but as I say it laid a foundation as solid as any created by Holmes and Sutcliffe, Hobbs and Sandham, Hutton and Washbrook, Hobbs and Rhodes. At that stage my partner relied on a terrific confidence, an unerring eye, no technique to speak of and a screaming golfer's swipe over mid-on's head from anything pitched on a length. (In the fullness of his days he has retained the confidence and the eye and added a technique, which dealt him over 1,000 runs in good club cricket every year for five successive seasons.) I, for my part, not yet coached into the impotent ortho-doxy which in good time succeeded in modifying everything but my hot-headed indiscrimination, had recourse to such random drives and slashes as the immediate needs of the moment dictated. I enjoyed it inordinately, whether taking convulsive avoiding action from the path of one of Victor's tee-shots or running half-way down the pitch to drive over the bowler's head and just failing to hole out down deep extra cover's throat. From that day, so far as I was concerned, he and I were for all cricket purposes as good as in-separable; and allowing for the natural hazards of adult life and circumstance, that stand has yet to be broken. On the intensity and quality of my appreciation of cricket its influence cannot be exaggerated.

Together we journeyed up the predatory ladder of school cricket. Initiates and addicts, the severe coaching and disciplining, to which every infant in that Junior School was submitted almost whether he liked it or not, did not irk us. Most of it we did not need, being well conditioned already by our temperaments; the rest we assimilated unthinkingly, not pausing to consider how painful the process must have been for subjects less willing to be drilled. Together we assented to the unwritten assumptions about cricket that our pastors and masters were enthusiastically bent upon inculcating; we did not chafe, but now I think we can realize that we retained sufficient detachment to be able to smile, a trifle wryly, at such standards and such values being permitted. When the M.C.C. sent down their annual side to play the School (the Senior School, of course), the Junior School was ordered into the cricket field to watch, as if it had been just another history lesson. We were assembled beforehand and given a pep talk about behaviour; noise, chattering, ragging and all natural concomitants of a relaxed afternoon in the sun were forbidden on pain of unmentionable penalties. Straggling about in the neighbourhood of the bowling screen was to be the finally unpardonable sin. " The M.C.C.," said the headmaster in a tone of hushed reverence as if he were saying the B.V.M., " the M.C.C. would naturally not tolerate such behaviour." We took it in, little innocents, we took it in. The Lord bless and preserve me, I took it in too. Without pausing to inquire for one healthy moment who the M.C.C. presumed to think it was, tolerating or not tolerating the behaviour of school-boys on their own ground where the M.C.C. was playing as a guest, we swallowed it all and went on to the cricket field as into Notre-Dame de Chartres, muscle-bound with worship, apprehensive with contrived tension; desperate and fearful lest the M.C.C., a random collection of half-pay officers, stockbrokers, university graduates with college 2nd XI colours and an overworked and disgruntled professional sucking a straw, should in its profound authority and wisdom do other than graciously tolerate our behaviour.

We swallowed this and we swallowed much beside; we were admirable cricket automata, with perhaps a hint of madness added which vitiated the organized effect of the training. Victor and I voyaged up together; in time we won our junior 1st XI colours, I as an opening batsman not without his moments, he, who had temporarily let his serious batting go, as a fastish bowler of a full and destructive power. Our fortunes fluctuated a little in the later years; although, when we went into the Senior School, he made the House eleven before I did, he never in the later reaches of our time at school did himself full justice. He was troubled with a ricked back and lost his penetrative power as a bowler; his batting maturity had not yet come on him. Although we made the 1st XI together, and ultimately (after some trials) the longed-for colours, I was luckier in my school cricket than he, who left a year earlier and could not enjoy the serenity and fruitfulness of a third year in the team. After schooldays our fortunes changed, and he has played far more regularly and far more successfully than I. He has battered his way into the M.C.C. in his own right as a player, and takes time off on occasion from his fabulously prosperous business to go down and play against schools. I can trust him, I think, to tolerate to the limits of his amiable disposition the behaviour of little boys press-ganged into watching a game they neither like nor understand.

But our journey through school cricket was unimportant compared with our other joint activities connected with the game. One of its culminations, for me, was the intense happiness and vividness of my last season in the school eleven, but it was a minor culmination and Victor did not share it. Rigorously as we were coached, by precept and practice, word and gesture, selflessly, tirelessly, by ageing masters with theories absorbed in the late nineties and worn threadbare to their graves; crippling as was the amount of cricket we had, age-long the hours and games we played, of all standards and of all kinds; nevertheless these activities but scratched the surface of our awareness of and consuming passionate interest in the vital heart of the game itself. This we fostered in our leisure hours. That we had any such to foster it in is a standing source of wonderment to me at this end of the perspective of time. Yet looking back it seems to me that in spite of long net-practices after school, in spite of the necessity to absorb enough book-knowledge to scrape ourselves through the recurrent examinations (which, truth to tell, were often welcomed, as their time-tables might provide a sudden free half-day on which there might be a match on at Lord's or the Oval)—in spite of distractions which would worry an adult into ulcers in three months, we managed to find ample time to prosecute, at our own convenience and to our own dictation, our burning fixation on the game. We found space and elbow-room in a nearby recreation ground, with varying and rather difficult rules about casual cricket with a hard ball; but various energetic ingenuities of one kind or another circumvented that, and night after night until dusk, avoiding the eye of the unsympathetic park-keepers and courting the friendship of any who seemed human, we played and replayed this game, a small group of us never more than six or seven strong, until for energy, flexibility of movement, and complete familiarity with all its devilish and fascinating hazards, there were few to equal us among our own acquaintance. I have seldom known physical exhaustion, of the contented and reflective kind, so happily and intimately as I knew it for those few seasons of adolescence; an exhaustion leaving no morning hang-over, keen hunger and deep thirst most gratefully assuaged and duly renewed; the heat and the sweat got into our joints and lubricated them, the fierce routine exercise toned up the muscles to a superb temper. I do not remember any time in my life when I have consistently felt so well. And whenever in later years I have made runs, or caught catches, or in any way felt for a happy moment worthy of this game, I have laid the credit at the door, not of the decorous net-drill or the traditional lessons taught me on my way up the elevens, but of this ruthless, exhausting but ultimately untiring informal cricket, with the bumpy wicket and the composition ball, and the unwavering voluntary devotion reinforcing the effort.

In the intervals of violent exercise there was, naturally, incessant talk. Most of this was about county cricket, much, though less of it, about our own school affairs. Of our ferocious addiction to cricket-watching as distinct from cricket-playing I shall have much more to say later; of our own school affairs I have said a little already, and there is more to come in a moment. But in case we should find a single instant free, in case a hollow moment should happen along without provision being made for a discussion on cricket past or present, we devised for our more specialized moments, and primarily for the winter, one of those fantastic cricket games which in one form or another are played by most boys and which are an extraordinary tribute to the eternal fascination which it exerts upon the juvenile (and not only the juvenile) imagination.

Of course I had played on my own when much younger a species of cricket up against a wall, with scoring worked out by myself and methodically entered on sheets of paper. In this way I had played dozens of imaginary championship matches, but there was always a tendency, however much one guarded against it, to cheat to the advantage of one's favourites. Surrey always won; Hobbs never failed to make a large score. But the game that ultimately evolved from the maelstrom of Victor's imagination and mine was an indoor exercise played purely on paper, and protected by hazard against favouritism of any kind. It started with a pack of ordinary playing cards: this being found unsatisfactory, it had recourse to a roulette wheel, of all unexpected implements; and round this whirling talisman, all winter through and wet summer as well, spun the elaborately contrived fortunes of all our well-loved first-class cricketers. We played championship matches and Test matches, Gents and Players and Test trials and all the trimmings; we played the H's against the B's; we played the World against a scarifying set of invented names representing Mars. And when this sequence palled we had the best brainwave of all. We collected our own team, our Junior School 1st XI plus a few outriding friends and enthusiasts, and sent them out among the counties like a touring side. In a few weeks we played a complete season through with terrific attendant excitement and success; and then we sent ourselves voyaging with conspicuous éclat through Australia, South Africa and the West Indies. (India in those days was still *in futuro* as an international force.) The strain could not have been more pronounced or prolonged if we had really been playing these matches; only I must confess that if we had, the likelihood of my collecting 183 in the second Test against South Africa (as I contrived to do through the roulette wheel's kindly agency) would have been removed into lost limbo. We kept the scores and we kept the averages; we compiled exercise book after fat exercise book of detailed flowery description of the play as frightful as any penny-a-lining journalist could have perpetrated, full of phrases like " Mason was at his splendid best, achieving in particular a miraculous shot off Tate when he contrived to hit a six over square-leg's head off a very fast yorker," or " Buckingham contrived to beat both Hobbs and Hammond by sheer pace off the pitch and, with the score at only 15, took the wickets of both these batsmen in the course of two overs; the ball with which he bowled the latter pitched a few inches outside the off stump and knocked the leg stump out of the ground."

These terrible volumes still exist, and we both go hot and cold all over when we recall the loving care with which they were compiled, the countless hours spent on the composition, and (enduring evidence this of the last extreme of monomania) the pictures of first-class cricket teams, individual cricketers, and incidents from actual matches solemnly snipped from newspapers and from copies of the *Cricketer* and renamed and relabelled with the identities of ourselves and our fellows. I was especially jealous of Victor when he coolly appropriated for himself a particularly glamorous and dashing photograph of E. R. T. Holmes, a cricketer for whom we had at that time an overweening hero-worshipping affection. I stifled my rage and went modestly on with my task, which was filling in with little black spots the wide blank spaces in the seats in an excellent photograph of Lord's (taken, I suppose, on the truncated second day of a match between the Royal Marines and the Royal Corps of Signals) preparatory to inscribing it with the bold legend: "SECOND TEST MATCH *v*. ENGLAND; R. C. MASON HITS TATE THROUGH THE COVERS FOR FOUR."

These frenetic activities continued with small sign of abatement for the best part of three years. They were, no doubt, harmless enough even in their most extravagant manifestations; they enlivened the long drabness of many winters and created fantasies which may have been infantile but which assumed no sinister directions or distortions. With the arrival of our middle teens outside preoccupations beckoned, and the flow slackened and died. There was the business of trying examinations to be faced, and the ever-present preoccupation of establishing a place in school cricket. In the increasing urgency the fantasies dimmed down.

They dimmed, but the interest itself never slackened. The creative activity, if you can call it that, merely shifted itself adroitly sideways. As I shall show later, its successor was as fantastic and as whole-hearted as these queer three years themselves had been; the one stemmed from the other and overbore it and outlived it. But the volumes remain, and the ridiculous accounts of matches that no one ever played, and scores we never achieved, and averages that never were on sea or land. Fools, but we also had our hour; the hour when Victor Buckingham bowled Hobbs and Hammond in consecutive overs on his own dining-room table, the hour when I and my trusty partner won the rubber at the Oval, guiding our side by a brilliant opening partnership to a ten-wicket victory. We too have lived in Arcadia; even if we had to build that visionary no-man's-land with our own bare hands.

There came a time when we returned, willingly enough, from our own Wonderland to the world of comparative reality that was (in the happy days of the late twenties) bounded by the hierarchies and routines of the school elevens. Once I had, a little luckily, entered the holy of holies, the 1st XI changing-room and all it implied, I never left it, keeping a tenuous and tentative place in the team for three of the pleasantest years of my life. Here the routine imposed upon us was a trifle less idiotic than it had been in the lower reaches, since we were all here of a standard to sympathize with it and to react in its favour and, do you see, to make it a little less necessary for the routine to be imposed at all; and we enjoyed the benefit of what had at the time the reputation, whether deserved or not I do not know, of being the finest wicket in Surrey outside the Oval, and a ground and outfield very much to match. As we advanced up the ladder, the pertinacities of the staff appeared to decrease in discipline and increase in sympathy; and the nagging routines of the lower reaches gave place to a concentrated series of specialized practices, including a vicious series of fielding exercises conducted by the captain, who had a wristy dexterity, on cold days, in hurling the ball at your head from six or eight yards' range. The batting and bowling were not now supervised so regularly by the masters as by the rheumaticky old professional, Bunyan by name, who had been a great friend of Jack Hobbs in the latter's early days at the Oval, and who was as kindly, friendly and sympathetic a coach as a nervy and unstable boy could wish to meet.

What I, what Victor, what anybody did in our seasons in school cricket do not matter; what interests me is the absorbed atmosphere that I spoke of earlier, the blinkered, fascinated concentration upon the progress of the season and the games that made it up. At the age of sixteen or seventeen, when the world, I suppose, should have been widening for me, it in fact narrowed intensely; during the summer, narrowed to a burning fanatical preoccupation which mercifully did not wholly stunt me. I am glad to remember that the lovely summer of 1929, my first in the Eleven, full of delectable memories of heat and drowsiness, of tingling small successes, of inconsequent snatches of tunes played on an old cracked gramophone in the pavilion (" Who?," " The Riff Song " from *The Desert Song*, and half a dozen more), is also knitted in my memory with the profounder glories of Theocritus, of *The Return of the Native*, of Rossetti, of Virgil. I do not find it inappropriate to recall their savour, which is still mine at any time for the asking, at the same time as I recall the more ephemeral pleasures of the cricket field. The one has lasted with me as long as the other.

And it was a lovely summer indeed. The novelty, the privileges, the spaciousness, all supplied their cumulative effect and gave the magic a rhythm and a vitality that have kept it living in the memory over twenty years and more. To miss morning prayers by special permission on match days while the Eleven changed in the pavilion, and to sit aloof and preoccupied during morning school with the air of having dropped in condescending-like until such time as more important matters should claim the attention; to leave school at the mid-morning break and start the game on the fresh, dewy green cricket field, cool and deserted with hardly a spectator; to hear in the distance the bells ring for the change of periods and to carry on grandly indifferent, to have the school pile out in a straggle at the lunch break to see how the Eleven was doing; to lunch, ourselves, in the high-windowed pavilion—I can taste the veal-and-ham pies to this day—eschewing the beer set out for our guests (save when our fast bowler waxed daring against the M.C.C., drank a forbidden pint, gave himself a frightful headache, and took three wickets in the first over after lunch); to play on, through afternoon school and out on the other side of it, until the shadows lengthened and the sunbeams struck in the yellow light; then showers, and banter enough, and home as best we could in the evening to chew over the immense implications of the match and to catch up desperately with arrears of work against the looming exams which yet were magically prevented from looming too horrifically. These were experiences deeply savoured at the time and even more deeply appreciated since, when the spaciousness that permitted these delights has, in the inevitable course of growth, vanished for ever.

There were the occasional away matches too, to which straw boaters had to be worn, and were lucky if they were not maliciously sat on during the journey; when we foregathered early and often did not come in to school at all, travelling far and wide by coach to distant corners of the Home Counties; to Epsom College, who provided the best lunch in all creation, and to the East Surrey Regiment at Kingston, whose officers' mess ran it very close; to Berkhamsted's windy tableland of a ground high on the Chiltern uplands, and to the superb historic greenness of the St. Lawrence ground at Canterbury, the only county ground on which I have ever played and where, to my eternal delight, I made some runs. At one such away match, at Perse School, Cambridge, on a day of unspeakable heat, a spectator was pointed out to me standing by the side of the pavilion, retired and remote, observing us with a contemplative air of melancholy, as well he might, since he was Tom Hayward; and this same match is ticketed happily in my memory for an epic altercation between our umpire Bunyan and the representative of our opponents, a burly, grumbling, red-faced old character whose son, we were told, had played for England. It all began with our excitable wicket-keeper, Bobby Brookes, a wicket-keeper adapted rather than born to the business, who took loud and vociferous pride in his success in the matter of stopping byes. Late in their innings, when his copybook was still unblotted, the ball flew to the boundary past his thrashing glove and their lugubrious umpire duly signalled four byes.

"Four more bloody byes," remarked Tubby Taylor from the slips, a cheerful opening batsman whom nothing could perturb.

"He hit it, you swine!" screamed the gyrating wicket-keeper amid happy laughter from all in the neighbourhood—except the lugubrious umpire, who conceiving in his warped, suspicious imagination that the exclamation had come from Bunyan (who would no more have been guilty of such a *gaffe* than of walking across a bowling screen) roared out, "You mind your own bloody business and I'll mind mine!"

"Who the hell are you shouting at?" inquired Bunyan, awakening from a sweltering contemplation of nothing at all (it was indeed an exceptionally hot day). "Silly old fool, I never said nothing; it was one of the boys."

"You mind your business down that end!" repeated the old man swelling truculently; "there's plenty to worry about down there without interfering with me, *I'm* sure," and he turned resentfully back to his job, utterly unpersuaded by the most careful and elaborate explanations that he had not been grossly and unpardonably insulted. For the rest of the day they coldly ignored each other; the old man mumbling and choking spasmodically, Bunyan darting contemptuous glances and muttering blasphemous comments as he stood at square-leg. The incident has lain dormant in my memory for years; rising occasionally to the surface it never fails to afford fresh and satisfying joys.

Coupled in my mind with this instantaneous vignette from my

first season in the Eleven is another more elaborately pleasing series
spread over the whole three years. This concerns our annual fixture
with the East Surrey Regiment, famed for its admirable cuisine;
during the three years of which I speak we visited them twice and
entertained them once. Their team was a congeries of immaculate
officers, subservient N.C.O.s, and crop-headed privates who were
treated with politeness as one treats a kitchen table with politeness.
Their opening bowler on the first occasion was a certain Private
Dogsbody or some such name, short and stocky with a face like a
deferential pug. His notion of opening the bowling was to run
briskly up to the wicket and get rid of the ball in a cathartic kind of
convulsion; length and direction were subordinate to speed. Tubby
Taylor, the cheerful opening batsman noticed above, made delighted
hay of this man's opening two overs; in ten glorious minutes more
than 30 runs were on the board, and the crestfallen Dogsbody was
marched off to some inconspicuous place in the outer darkness to
pull his socks up and watch his superiors go through the drill more
effectively. Time went on, and the scoring slowed; the substitute
bowler found a length and took a wicket here and there, and in due
order I arrived at the wicket to carry on the flagging task. I found
the bowling something more accurate and hostile than I would have
desired; I got a two here and a three there, but it was too defensive
a game for one of my random spirit, and I was beginning to flush
a delicate green with envy at the utterly undeserved good fortune
of the man Taylor in having been presented with all that flotsam
and jetsam at the very outset, when whom should I see once more
preparing to bowl but this same Private Dogsbody, who had by
now presumably worked his passage and been given parade-ground
instructions to pick 'em up and do it properly this time. My mouth
watered copiously at the prospect; I hugged myself with anticipatory delight, I looked round the field, spat on my hands, took a firm
and comfortable grip of the bat, and received a ball which pitched
just on or outside the line of the off-stump, broke back sharply
without making any kind of lift from the pitch, and despatched my
middle stump some way past the wicket-keeper, who was rather
injudiciously standing right up to the wicket. That was the only
wicket that the man Dogsbody took in the whole match.

I looked for him with interest the next year, and sure enough there he was. This time he was Lance-Corporal Dogsbody, and was full of life and bounce. Again he opened the bowling. Tubby Taylor took two terrific fours off the first two balls of the innings; Lance-Corporal Dogsbody bowled him comprehensively with the third. That was the only wicket that he took in the whole match.

On the last of the three occasions when we met this regimental team, rain prevented any play, and the good Dogsbody had no chance to introduce into the game his characteristic brand of fireworks. It is to be assumed, however, that he had not been idle in one direction or another during the intervening period; a Greek fate had pursued him and for what reason or with what ultimate effect on his story I shall probably never know, he was Private Dogsbody again. It is possible that he was guilty of some shocking misdemeanour, an unmentionable indiscipline; possible that he had merely, with that gross incompetence that was so plainly a part of his endearing nature, run his own captain out. He remains in the background of my life an attractive figure of fun, with that sudden unexpected potentiality for utter destructiveness never far from the engaging surface of his cricket.

These and other incidents, these and other characters, fill out the bare tale of my youth's preoccupations. Beginning, as we all begin, with the skeletal ritual of which I spoke at the very start of my narrative, I informed the game thus early with elements of character, of incident, and of atmosphere, which by the time I had arrived at any pretence of maturity had established it in my life as a kind of panoramic drama of graceful and exciting action, taking enrichment from human qualities and giving to its human devotees its new enrichment back. My early prep-school experiences had sharpened and ripened my interest in it, with the Wyatt episode adding a piquancy which I should be the poorer for having missed; my later adventures at my public school lent discipline and discrimination to my practice of the game, and established in me, for better or worse and once and for all, this ingredient of total absorption which is a boy's prerogative and a boy's only, which he can never hand on in full percentage to the man into whom he evolves. But he can hand on a part of it, a residual part that adult distractions cannot wholly disperse; and the cricketer who has been disinherited of this essential legacy is poor indeed. It does not consist in a desire to shut out maturity, a Peter Pan reluctance to accept the responsibilities of manhood; but only in a power to prolong even into senility the complete receptivity into which a boy can automatically attune himself when he sets forth to play this game. The true cricketer, even of middle age, carries into each match something (it may be only a shadowy something, but of its quality there is normally no mistake) of the dedicated freshness and integrity of the boy's total abandonment to the mystery and the delight. From my boyhood approach to it I took fantasy and fun, which added living romance to the living ritual; added to these from my years in the Eleven came both the practical importance and (vastly more significant) the deep memorable satisfaction of living and working as a team. This is not the team spirit of the common canting phrase; this is the hugely valuable experience of common achievement effected through a common endeavour. And when the endeavour and the achievement are so æsthetically and emotionally satisfying as these were, what wonder that I look back on them as seminal experiences affecting not only the future of my cricket but the future of my life? What more natural than that there are times when I could wish to renew the actuality; to breathe once more the untrammelled early morning air of pre-lunch play, to have that spacious field and those spacious and dispersed companions around me again, to come out once more from that pavilion into the sunshine with my partner, after lunch, 24 not out shall I say, two wickets down for 91 and the wicket hard and true, and not a care in my head about next week's examination or next year's job—nothing in the world but the bowling and the fielding to hinder me, and a whole summer's afternoon at my mercy?

CHAPTER FOUR

SURREY TRIUMPHANT

ALL my life I have been a Surrey man. I was born in the county not far from one of its richest tracts of pine-wood; I spent my boyhood almost within sight of its dry coniferous heaths bedded in sand; I went to school there, and apart from temporary interludes in London and in wartime exile, that is where I grew and where I grow. The county itself has many forthright critics, who complain of its strangling urbanization and snobbish gentility. There are moments when I agree with much of what they say; but I only have to take a walk in the village which is now my home, or go southward through the woods and commons to the line of the North Downs, from where I can range over half a hundred miles of wooded pasture-land and trace the hunched rise of the heights to the Devil's Punch Bowl and beyond, to acknowledge the intense lasting beauty that abides in my home county. Even the knowledge that my certainty is three parts selfish pride and possessive obstinacy will not avail to shake it. All my life I have been, and I rather hope that all my life I shall be, a Surrey man.

In a cricket sense Surrey is of course urban. The Oval is so conspicuously ungraceful a ground as to have acquired a certain distinctive quality in its plainness. The word "Surrey" for me conjures up bracken and tanglewood, pine trees and downland gaps, beech and birch and heather; its cricket is not of this quality at all, neither are its cricketers, and I hasten to say that I mean this as no reflection upon them or upon the cricket they play. Some counties carry around with them a distinctive regional flavour. I need mention no more than the name of Yorkshire; while in a subtly evocative way I have known no county, in the persons of its representative elevens, exude such a characteristic aroma as Sussex. The tan on a Sussex cricketer seems always to be pitched several shades deeper and darker than that on a cricketer of a less favoured county; it was a wonderful sight at the turn of the twenties and thirties, at Hove with the sun shimmering on the sea and the breeze coming up from the prom, to see Tate, Bowley, the Parkses and the Langridges and the Cornfords, and if your memory were comprehensive and elastic the Gilligans, the Oakeses and the Coxes, with the sea glare on their faces and the deep tan all over them wherever they showed, burned a gorgeous orange by the Sussex sun, an orange that seemed ingrained as if it had been rubbed in with sea salt. Even at Lord's and the Oval they carried with them the good earth of their engendure; on Bank Holiday at Lord's in June you could almost smell the spray off the breakers when they came out to field. I have for this curious associative reason retained always a soft spot for Sussex; but though the men of Surrey imply no such adventitious delights, being associated in the minds of the whole outside world with a gasworks, and in the minds of everyone who has watched at the Oval (with the wind in the right direction) with the brewery next to Victoria Station, it is to the men of Surrey, and the county they represent, that I have given my loyalty.

My father was an expatriate Lancastrian, who had come early in life to work humbly and hard—a characteristic of his whole self-denying existence—in the London Civil Service, in which before he died he attained distinction, though not high enough for his quality. Deeply fond of cricket, he had played himself and given much thought to the game, but family responsibilities fought with the rarer preoccupation in his honourable and conscientious mind, and the family responsibilities won hands down. He played no cricket when I knew him; and virtually he watched none either, except school matches in which I was playing. I was a full member of Surrey for more than six years during his lifetime, with the power to give him a more comfortable day at the Oval than he had ever enjoyed in his life; yet I could never persuade him to come with me. I have wondered since whether he harboured under a quiet undemonstrative exterior a cherishing tenderness of the past that prevented him from repairing to the matches of the Southern folk. He was not on the surface a man to whom poetry made much appeal; but it may be that, towards the end of his life at any rate, he found the field for him too full of shades. The last time when to my knowledge he spent a full day at the Oval he saw his home county, Lancashire, bat all day on a plumb wicket against what was at the time notorious for being the weakest bowling side in England. Lancashire made over 500, Ernest Tyldesley made over 200, and I have no doubt there were lashings of Makepeace and Hallows and Watson as well. I was furious at the time, and although I cannot remember doing so, I probably cried (I was, I think, eight years old). But my father had had a good day, and I think he never forgot its pleasure, though he lived on many years into the era of Washbrook and Paynter, whom he never saw. A quiet solid supporter of Lancashire, the quietest and most unassuming I have ever met, he appreciated and fostered my Surrey loyalty, and never obtruded his own.

He it was who first showed me how a score-book was set out and completed; and he chose to fill out a blank sheet with an imaginary innings of the then Surrey eleven. At this late date, thirty-three years after, I revere his forbearance in not making it Lancashire; had he done so, it may be that all my allegiances would have been different. The Surrey eleven began, I remember, as it always did then and seemed as if it always would, with Hobbs, Sandham, Ducat and Shepherd, in that magical and irreversible order, and it ended up (I can see the page now, in my father's neat handwriting) Hitch, Strudwick, Rushby. The order of the interveners I cannot remember, but they comprised, I think, P. G. H. Fender, Peach and W. J. Abel for certain, and one other dim and barely remembered figure who may have been Harrison. And these neat hieroglyphs on paper, some of which were already faintly familiar to me and some of which I saw then (solemn thought) for the very first time in the world, became almost at once symbolic of great misty legendary figures in a world of great excitement and importance; and from that time onward I read the scores in the papers with a close interest, welcoming Hobbs, Sandham, Ducat and Shepherd as familiar friends when I encountered them in print, and soon putting labels of potentiality and prowess on to all the others. Surrey, from half-way through that season of 1920 (I seem to have begun taking an interest bang in the middle of the season through no discoverable cause), were " my county "; on my behalf these heroic names that I knew so well on paper strove and succeeded, strove and failed,

battled their way to within sight of the championship until they
were gloriously beaten by Middlesex at Lord's in the crowning
culmination of Plum Warner's last unbelievable season of success.
When Plum Warner beat Surrey that day, he beat me too; and
still they were only names.

At the very beginning of the very next season my father immersed
me in the seventh heaven of delight by taking me for the first time
in my life to the Oval. I was passionately excited about this; I can
still sense the steadying moderation of my father's conduct of the
whole affair, a temperate man controlling a fantastically intemperate
small boy. He may have guessed that more than thirty years later
I would remember certain incidents and scores and personalities of
this trivial game far more clearly than I retain the salient impressions
of matches in which I played myself last July; he was kindly
and interested and indulgent; I do not know if he knew that
he was launching a blazing fanatic into the heart of his life-long
fanaticism.

The match was so unimportant as to be laughable; it was a Surrey
trial match. To my recollection there was a sizeable enough crowd;
we got there after lunch on the second day, taking a tram from
Vauxhall Station because my father had forgotten how short the
walk was from there to the entrance gate. (That shows how little
he had been there; he told me that he saw a Gents and Players
match there in 1893 on the wedding-day of the Duke and Duchess
of York, later King George V and Queen Mary; apart from that I
know of no definite visit he had ever paid to the place.) We sat by
the scoreboard beneath the great gasometer, and on that day we saw
in the flesh all the bearers of those legendary names who were
already established in my imagination. When we arrived, the
unmistakable figure of Percy Fender, balding, moustachioed,
elongated, was at the crease; at the other end was the left-handed
Bill Cook, against whom generations later I played in several
Departmental matches. Cook's was the first wicket I ever saw fall
at the Oval; I still remember the roar as he touched an outswinger
into the wicket-keeper's gloves—I had never really heard an appeal
before. My father identified my heroes for me; Hobbs at cover, a
twinkling-footed Sandham on the boundary, a rubbery cherubic
Peach bowling. Not unnaturally I concentrated on Hobbs, who

early on missed a catch, to my consternation and I think my father's as well; he looked much like anyone else, a trifle thicker set than I had expected, and lacked the heroic air of massive distinction that his reputation seemed to have earned him. Only when Fender failed to get hold of an off-drive and gave him a running catch which he took without difficulty did we discover from the figures on the score-board that he wasn't Hobbs at all; that the great man had strained his leg and was not in view; and that the mere mortal who had usurped immortality was a modest amateur who (I later learned) was an admirable character-actor called Desmond Roberts. This was probably the only time in his life when he played the lead without knowing it.

Of the rest of the afternoon I have fleeting glimpsed memories; of G. M. Reay, who bowled in pince-nez (fifteen years later he bowled at me, and through no fault of my own did not get me out); of the friendly Strudwick and the cheers that greeted him; of the immense and ubiquitous energy of Peach; of the roaring welcome to Bill Hitch. This worthy had a most memorable innings; he prodded vaguely at his first ball, and loosed off an almighty flailing drive at his second. This climbed heavens higher than the pavilion, and the crowd gasped and chattered as it sailed into the invisible; and when it came down it came down into the hands of Sandham, imperturbable on the pavilion rails. There was also, perhaps most eccentric of all, a lob bowler, Molony by name, who had blown the top off the banner headlines in the evening papers by inducing Hobbs to be stumped off his bowling in the first innings. The crowd laughed itself into an apoplexy when he bowled; but I think he took some wickets that day as well. He turned out for the county in a match or two later in the season, with little success. These, and Sandham's beautiful economical quickness of foot when he batted, are the enduring treasures that this crowded and important afternoon at this far from crowded and far from important match stored permanently in my memory; but even the ecstasy of the whole marvellous experience could not compensate for the failure of Desmond Roberts to be Hobbs.

Later that season we went for our holiday within striking distance of Brighton; where, in the space of a couple of weeks, I crowded in two notable experiences—George Hirst bowling for

Yorkshire, and Gregory and Macdonald bowling for Armstrong's Australians. But these are extraneous memories of a ground that for a year or two was more familiar to me than any, even the Oval; and it was nearly two years before I saw Surrey in a championship match. My father could not take me to that one, which was against Essex; but much to my surprise, and I rather think to hers, my mother did—under whose persuasion, and with what intensity of patient self-sacrifice, I can hardly begin to conjecture. This time I really saw Hobbs, though not to any very satisfactory extent, as he was l.b.w. to his old enemy Johnny Douglas for 20, ten of which he had made the night before, and my mother equates to this day the idea of deadly stodgy batsmanship and the pointless drudgery of first-class cricket with the name of Shepherd, that honest and reliable yeoman-batsman who anchored Surrey's middle batting for a dozen years, and whose sterling 40 or so on this June morning of 1923 did so much to retrieve his county's rather rickety fortunes. Fender made over 50, and Peach rather laughably had a stump knocked out of the ground second ball; and that is about all that I can recall of this my first full introduction to my county, except that to my intense agony and embarrassment my mother knitted placidly all day.

I encountered Surrey at the beginning of a time of transition. In the last year before the First World War they had won the championship for the first time since 1899, running to the top of the table in the last few weeks of July 1914 when everybody was too preoccupied to notice. Of that 1914 side, Hobbs, Sandham, Fender, Strudwick, Rushby, Hitch, Ducat, and others as well, took up the effort again when play was resumed. They were joined for a short time by J. N. Crawford and, for a scintillating season or two, by Donald Knight. A few years after the war, an Oxford Blue of unusual maturity and quality named Jardine joined the team for certain intermittent matches. With this terrific array of names you would have thought that championship honours would have been ready for the asking, whether they had any worthy rivals or not. But during the few years when this magnificent collection of genius and talent were still available and in strength, certain injections of bad luck combined with sudden accessions of youth and adventurousness in other counties, notably Middlesex and Yorkshire.

R. E. S. WYATT
PLAYING HIS
FIRST BALL FROM
GRIMMETT IN
THE TEST MATCH
AT THE OVAL,
1930.

"How Wyatt got
through that last
horrifying over before
tea is part of his
story, not of mine. . . ;
he remembers it in
horrible detail as one
of the most harrowing
experiences of his life."

(p. 39)

Above: JACK HOBBS SCORING THE HUNDREDTH RUN OF THE CENTURY WITH WHICH HE EQUALLED W. G. GRACE'S RECORD, TAUNTON, AUGUST, 1925. (*p. 83*)

Below: HOBBS AND SANDHAM COMING OUT TO BAT AT THE OVAL ON THEIR FIRST APPEARANCE AFTER HOBBS HAD BEATEN GRACE'S RECORD, AUGUST, 1925. (*p. 104*)

Hendren, Hearne, Stevens, Haig and Allen in the one, and Holmes, Sutcliffe, Macaulay, Robinson, Waddington, Kilner and Leyland in the other, were, on the whole, younger than Surrey's leading cricketers and, on the way up to triumphs, met the ageing Surrey combination on the way down. Before I had watched Surrey half a dozen times, Rushby was gone and Hitch was gone, Crawford had disappeared altogether and Knight's glorious achievements had begun to sputter and fizzle and fail. Jardine's day was yet to come; and another amateur, Jeacocke, had too little reliability to make up for these dangerous erosions.

On the credit side—I suppose it was the credit side—was the marvellous Oval wicket, the death of a succession of would-be fast bowlers. The Oval wicket today is an entirely different affair, cunningly contrived to take spin at an early stage and crack up convincingly at the latter end; but in the twenties it was like concrete. Bill Hitch banged and grunted away at the Vauxhall end, but even he could hardly get the ball to stump height; and in the fifth Test in Armstrong's destroying series Philip Mead took a record score off Gregory and Macdonald without any apparent fuss or difficulty. This wicket naturally favoured the powerful Surrey batting; and what opposing sides must have felt, coming down the steps into the mid-morning sunlight having lost the toss on a fine Saturday and having (let us say) no very penetrating attack, knowing that they would presently be followed to the middle by Hobbs and Sandham, with Ducat, Shepherd, Knight, Jardine, Fender and Peach to tag along behind, it is possible to guess but it has not gone on record. What is, conversely, also possible to guess is the meditation of the Surrey captain in similar plight, with, say, Holmes and Sutcliffe or Makepeace and Hallows on the way to the wicket and nobody to open the bowling but himself and Peach. Hobbs could get a hundred every time he went in, and Sandham and Shepherd could be relied on for at least another one between them, and scores of 500 and 600 by Surrey were not so much irregularities but accentuations of the usual—but the melancholy truth could not be avoided: that with an attack consisting largely of a brisk medium-pace bowler who laughed all over his face and could occasionally swing the new ball, and of the infinite but qualitatively various wiles of a clever captain who bowled so much because there was no one else, the team would not only fail to collect the championship but should consider themselves lucky if they won any matches at all. And it was true enough that on the rare occasions when their batting faltered, as it often did against Kent at Blackheath, their besetting weakness let them in for some terrible drubbings. The introduction towards the end of the twenties of such thrustful amateur talent as Errol Holmes and Maurice Allom did little to assuage the desert atmosphere; the first sight of salvation, though I must confess that on a superficial view it took some long while to resemble it, was the arrival of a lumbering and gangling young fast bowler from somewhere in South London, who kneed and elbowed his way in due time to fame, respect, an England cap, and an illustrious position among the game's great coaches and oracles—Alf Gover.

But in my salad days he was still very much a thing of the future, and Surrey still buoyed themselves up as best they could in the championship table on the strength of their transcendent batting. For myself, in my purblind partisanship, I worried less about this than I should have. I came to this game as a batsman; or rather, should I say, as one inclined to concentrate on batting rather than on bowling. When I watched a match my heart and sympathies were mainly with the batsman, though local and national loyalties would naturally create exceptional cases here. Therefore it was natural enough that Surrey's batsmen had all my joy and support, that nothing pleased me better than to read in the paper or to hear on the radio Surrey 527 for 6: Hobbs 114, Sandham 138, Jardine not out 106—and this was no rarity, it occurred on an average once a fortnight; the fact that it was almost invariably followed by a failure to get rid of their opponents twice or (not infrequently) even once, was in my shortsighted ecstasy completely overlooked. And the dispassionate spectator might perhaps have been forgiven for assuming that the groundsman and the committee at the Oval had overlooked it too. Life at the Oval was a batsman's paradise; it carried within its implications all the ingredients of a fool's paradise as well.

Fool or not, I did not mind. I basked contentedly in the happy glories of those prodigious scores, I visualized (I, whose highest score in any cricket was at that time 42) the weary satisfaction of the batsmen as they achieved yet another century partnership, yet another double hundred, yet another total soaring above the 550 mark. I spared no thought for Fender's worries, as, padded to go in Number 7 in the cool of the evening to thrash a cheap 60 or 70 out of a shattered attack, he considered for a moment (and considerably more than a moment, I suspect) what kind of a vengeance the opposing batsmen were contemplating for the morrow. Fender's tenure of the Surrey captaincy, one of the cleverest and least-rewarded by higher recognition in the history of the first-class game, must have held for him many doubts and problems, as he used his surpassing astuteness to shuffle a collection of honest bowlers with hardly a bite or bounce among them into the semblance of a workable attacking combination. He had to use himself as three or four different types of bowler in turn; he had to make Peach look like an opening bowler; he had to overbowl Shepherd, a genuine trier if ever one lived, who did not look as if he could remove my senior house captain, much less Woolley or Philip Mead. When the amateurs came down from the universities he used them all he could; but even they, except Allom, were stronger with the bat than with the ball. Fender just had to bash on regardless of the weakness, and hope it was temporary; it is to his immense credit that Surrey remained, throughout this period of lop-sided grandeur, a powerful side, to be reckoned with the strongest. It is doing a collection of admirable cricketers no injustice to declare that Surrey's batting in the twenties depended largely on Hobbs and Sandham with highly competent, indeed formidable, auxiliaries; the bowling simply depended on Fender.

The Surrey team in the twenties, for all its imperfections, became without knowing it my very good friends and familiars. They made a homely and comforting picture, coming out of the pavilion gate in their chocolate caps—a colour I have always taken to, for its associations both gastronomic and gasometrical—Fender at the head, tall, lean, with bowed baldish head and spectacles, hawk-like nose over tufted moustache, silk scarf and elongated sweater that he wore to please the cartoonists; Hobbs following, dark and thought-ful, with a trim light step that revealed a perfect poise both of body and mind; little Strudwick with bared grinning teeth and outsize pads, going grey; bow-legged Peach with the round humorous face and the blacksmith's arms, hatless and smiling; Andy Ducat, handsome and twinkling like one's favourite uncle, who years later was to drop dead in the middle of an innings at Lord's; Sandham, aloof and withdrawn, stepping as delicately as Agag to third man, economical in gesture, watchful, Oriental, impeccably neat; burly Shepherd with the brick-red moon-face and the Surrey cap he never removed in any circumstances whatever, shoulders like a bull and temperament as placid and pleasant as a good garden vegetable. Among these gleamed exotically here and there a Harlequin cap; Knight, Jardine, Errol Holmes, perhaps; and modestly in the rear would come some slight uncapped youngster on trial as a bowler, soon to vanish into night again after a fierce trial on that beast of a wicket, or as a batsman, to substitute for an injured regular and to relapse once more into obscurity when the first-line man came back. Sometimes one of these would take root, become for me an acceptable part of the familiar scene, grow into the usual group and set himself into a necessary foundation for use when these friends could no longer continue to court our welcome day after day; of these were Barling, squarely confident with a broad bat and mature manner, and a fleetfoot, lean, prematurely balding young athlete called Bob Gregory, featherweight and active, a cricketer of lissom and graceful talent who in good time grew capable and popular in the service of Surrey and England.

There they walked, the Surrey men, to take their places in the field; Strudwick baring his teeth behind the wicket, Shepherd and Fender in the slips, Gregory policing one outfield and Sandham another, Hobbs by royal and undisputed prerogative guarding the covers. They were patchy and brilliant by turns, flooring catches all over the place on days when the world spun the wrong way for them, achieving the impossible on others. Fender snapped up beauty after beauty in the slips; easier ones he would sometimes put down, and his colleague Shepherd was what they call " safe " rather than " brilliant " in all weathers. Hobbs at his best—though when I came to see him he was slowing up—was said to be the greatest cover-point in the game, with an underhand flick like a cracking rifle-bullet and a sure hand for any catch that was going; I saw him once catch Jack Hearne off a slash at a wide long hop, bang off the middle of the bat and humming as it climbed; Hobbs leaped as it screamed over him, flung up his left hand and caught it, and instantly jerked it up and away over his head in a rocketing swoop of abandon, almost before Hearne knew he was out. In that instantaneous expert reaction I caught my most vivid glimpse of his extraordinary mobility, which his lithe silent strolling motion so generally concealed.

Sandham in his earlier days could run round the boundary like a whippet, and I never saw him miss a catch; not even the fearful steam-hammer clump that the vast Barratt of Notts unloosed off the hardworking but unsuccessful slow bowler Fenley one day, which Sandham backing on to the pavilion rails misjudged late in its flight but caught desperately one-handed with back-bent elbow somewhere about the lobe of his right ear. But the most concise example of Surrey unreliability was provided by Errol Holmes in a match against Middlesex. Deep at extra cover he made a convulsive grab at a swirling mis-hit from the Hon. C. N. Bruce, that beautiful stylist, and took it on the end of his finger. He picked the ball from the carpet, slung it back and wrung his bruised hand meaningfully, gesturing at Fender that he was bleeding to death and wished to retire for repairs. Fender peremptorily waved him back to his place, whether as a punishment for having dropped the catch or because he wanted to get the over finished first was not clear; and at the very next ball Bruce unleashed a glorious high drive over mid-off's head, which the breeze retarded a little in its flight for Holmes to take superbly with one outstretched hand as he sprinted all out along the rails. Then Fender let him go to be tended in peace; a bit of good luck with all the air of a master-stroke of captaincy.

They return to me in dreams, these men of Surrey of my early and indiscriminate years, a group of cricketers enlarged by memory into a kind of statuesque greatness. It is not much wonder, knowing their history, that I think of them mainly at the wicket, rather than at their pertinacious but mediocre bowling or at their bright erratic antics in the field. I think most readily and naturally of Hobbs and Sandham; but this is part of a specialized study, an advanced consideration of genius that will take longer than a paragraph and which ranges over wider borders than my own county's; I think of the sturdy and elegant Ducat with his air of friendly humorous distinction, making good for so many long afternoons the bases and corner-stones of these fantastically long scores. Shepherd, too, comes back much to mind, with a free, clean off-driving style that took him once into a Test trial at Lord's; and how out of place his sunburnt honest figure with its chocolate cap looked there on that cloistral greensward among the England colours. He was born for Surrey and he lived and worked for Surrey, but obediently he travelled to Lord's to play in this important game and obediently he bowled and fielded, and obediently in due time he went forth to bat, a big fish out of water. That he proceeded to engage with Leyland in a stand of over 200, driving beautifully and seeming never for a moment at a loss with the wiliest bowlers in the kingdom, never surprised me for a moment; that his innings of 90 or so was very correctly singled out as one of the gems of the match was entirely right and proper and to be expected. That the selectors would never do anything about it, or that he would never get his chance to appear in any other representative matches of any kind, was almost as inevitable a corollary; and Tom Shepherd from that time forth obediently and I do not doubt quite contentedly continued to bat and bowl at the Oval, where he was known and honoured and knew his way about.

Peach follows him in my memory, with great hammering cow-shots belabouring all and sundry, much beloved of the schoolboys and cut out to the same pattern as they; but it is Fender to whom, of the later batsmen, is owing the greatest debt of all Surrey spectators, a player of great courage and resource and unpredictable genius, who had the capacity, fairly liberally displayed, to turn a game inside out in half an hour if his caprices and the Fates were in favour of it. He had an immense reach and he could hit like a flail; he once made 113 in thirty-five minutes at the Oval, that vastest of spaces, and he hit higher and farther than anyone else I have ever seen perform on that ground, save only Frank Mann and Frank Woolley. Hobbs or no Hobbs, it would be unfair to Fender to deny him the honour; if one man were to be called out of the past to represent the essential virtues of Surrey in the twenties, of speaking and acting and batting and bowling and fielding and captaining, half a side embodied in one man, my choice would be Fender, and if I were to nominate him I believe that Hobbs would leap to be the seconder.

And it is perhaps because of Fender's central and essential part in it that I remember as the most fascinating and characteristic day's play that Surrey ever provided me with in those remote twenties a certain Monday early in the school holidays, when the sky was blue with summer and the sun and all Heaven lay about us newly released to enjoy the last full month of cricket as it was intended to be enjoyed; with Surrey and Kent—a Kent before the late unhappy debilitation set in—matched genius for genius and talent for talent on this same Oval of all our obsessed delight. Confessedly on the Monday morning the Surrey genius seemed sadly in eclipse, since they had been caught by Freeman on an aftermath of rain on the Saturday, had been swept out for 131 before the wicket dried out, and had already been headed, and well headed, before the weekend had even begun. Most mercifully Woolley was out late on Saturday night, but with 160 on the board only four wickets were down, with the dangerous Ames still batting. And the Monday morning lent little relief in the beginning, for Gover in his nonage was cracked hither and thither by Ames, and Fender played the three-card trick with his dog's-eared attack to no purpose at all. It was left to the optimistic Garland-Wells to charm Legge into snicking a catch to slip; but the fifth wicket did not fall until Kent were over 120 ahead, and Ames putting bat to ball with that square crisp vigour that was for nearly a whole generation such a refreshment to see.

The turning point came when Hobbs gathered his forty-five years about him like a mantle and threw Ames out from cover, a manoeuvre he was prone to repeat even when he was fifty-two and creaking at the knees. Ames was four short of his hundred and had seemed unbowlable; the shock to him communicated itself to his county, and Fender and Garland-Wells rolled up the tail with expert dispatch for the addition of only 30 runs. Nevertheless Surrey faced a tidy deficit of 151 runs as they went to lunch, and I can well visualize the behaviour of a modern pair of openers at such a crucial stage. Let the runs come, don't take risks, for God's sake don't get out, stay in at all costs till tea-time, don't hook till your fifty's up, on no account try to cut while the shine's on, let 'em alone on the off, let 'em alone on the leg, put your pads to the inswings, watch the googly—you can hear the advice materialize out of the upper air, and see the batsmen shape accordingly. It is therefore with a nostalgia half regretful that I record that Hobbs calmly helped himself to 13 off the opening over, including three consecutive fours, crack, crack, crack, just like that. That was his way, and there was no gainsaying him. I know that Kent's opening bowlers were not conspicuously destructive, but I have seen him treat Macdonald just the same.

Hobbs cut the openers into strips and was very little dismayed by the arrival of Freeman, though it is true that Freeman slowed him down. Anchored to reality by a succession of admirably modest and temperate partners, Sandham, Ducat, Shepherd, who each remained with him for fifty or sixty runs and then unobtrusively departed, he saw the considerable deficit off in one of the most brilliant and delightful innings that I have ever been lucky enough to see. He batted as if he were playing an exhibition innings in a charity match against token bowlers; not as if he were conducting his county up a serious, indeed a critical, hill against Freeman and Marriott, two of the best spin bowlers in England. He got to his hundred in a series of bewildering boundaries; and just as the time looked ripe for a consolidating attack on the bowling, to make good the hard-won advantage, he followed his usual plan of relaxing after the century and was caught off a sliced drive. Surrey were still a beggarly 40 or so ahead; and in a horrid few minutes down tumbled the wickets of Garland-Wells, Barling and Gregory, and Surrey had let slip the strenuous gain once more.

This is where Fender abode most signally in the breach. Aided by the beefy Peach, who gaily hoicked his agricultural way through the subtlest of Marriott's mysteries, Fender deployed against the intelligence of these formidable slow bowlers a cunning dexterity that was more than their match. He did not go in for his usual game of spit on the hands and slosh; he lay back and cut, he went up on his toes for the wristy deflection, he farmed the bowling and ran between the wickets like an overgrown tarantula eager for prey. These two added forty invaluable runs in as many minutes; and when the inevitable happened and Peach hit under a ball from Freeman and sliced it into the upper air, the tenuous lead had stretched to a full hundred and Fender was still in control.

Yet 100 was not much. Kent had a full day to play with, Surrey's bowling was what we know it was, and Kent led off with Hardinge and Ashdown before unleashing the Olympian enormities of Woolley and Ames; not to mention light-weight hangers-on like Legge and Valentine. In those days Kent were a far-reaching and far-destroying menace, and Fender, contemplating from the non-striker's end the arrival of the jaunty Brooks, Strudwick's acrobatic and entertaining successor, must have wondered just how much more rope he could pay out. Brooks, an individual of inscrutable temper, of high executive competence behind the wicket and of disturbing instability in front of it, got his head down that day and played the innings of his life. He plonked an uncompromising dead bat in the front of the most innocuous of Freeman's tempters; he held up one end while Fender streaked into brilliant attack at the other. Brooks' tactics, far too subtle for certain ignorant pot-heads about the refreshment bars, called forth deplorable barracking in some quarters, a sinful display of illiteracy and bad taste; but he didn't care, he waved cheerfully and went on stodging, and when Fender and Gover were finally shot out in three balls, nearly forty more runs had been added of which the good Brooks had scored one in half an hour, and Kent were left with about 130 to get with five minutes of the day remaining in which to get started.

What Fender or any other Surrey man thought of the chances is not on record. They were certainly better than they had been; but for Hobbs, Fender and the sterling sheet-anchors at the top of the order, Surrey would already have been defeated and back in the pavilion; and it was mainly the resource and energy of Fender that had seen them as far from defeat as, for the moment, they were. And even the one over that was bowled that night to Hardinge was a proof of his irrepressibility; for he bowled it himself and the very first ball whipped off the edge of a groping bat into Peach's hands in the gully. It spoils a beautiful story, and it deeply pains me to have to set it down, that Peach put it promptly on the carpet; and in that wild flurry of excitement, which took our minds temporarily off the ease with which the Kent batsmen would tomorrow knock off the paltry 130 or so that Surrey had set them, this most stirring and characteristic day of a fine side in their full variety and glory came to a fitting close. I did not go to the Oval next day, and so I cannot describe it now; but Fender and Peach, tails up and the devil take the pack of you, bowled out the pride of Kent before lunch and nudged Surrey home to victory by 14 runs. There were giants in those days; and not the least of them were playing at the Oval, under the eyes of an avid small boy who cherished the memory all his life.

Let that recollection stand as the active epitome of the virtues and the graces of the Surrey cricket into which I grew up. It was the evening of the great day of Fender's eleven; this match was played in 1928, and at the turn of the thirties the familar constituents began to disintegrate. Strudwick had already gone; Ducat and Peach followed; Shepherd departed a year or two later. Even Fender himself, handing for a year or so the captaincy to Jardine, became no longer a fixture but an intermittent welcome instillation of life into a set of decaying memories. Hobbs and Sandham seemed for a time as immortal as Castor and Pollux; but imperceptibly, sadly, inevitably, they faded too. When Errol Holmes began his vigorous years of captaincy in the middle thirties there had been a very clean sweep indeed; the robust and proficient Fishlock, a maturing Barling and a highly competent Gregory, now shared most of the batting with the equable Squires as Hobbs and Sandham faded from the picture. Spasmodically an erratic Freddie Brown blazed his way to a memorable hundred or bowled out half a side of Test batsmen, then lapsed into ineffectiveness, Northamptonshire and England stirring in grumbling futurity far within his considerable fame; a lanky all-rounder called Parker assisted an energetic Watts and a more purposeful Gover in the strengthening of the attack. Right up to 1939 this reconstructed eleven, full of talent but never somehow able to realize itself as a powerful combination as under Fender, revealed exemplary competence without ever recalling to actuality the great character with which the Oval in the twenties had been so attractively bedecked.

The glory had, I suppose, as it always does, departed. I was no longer a schoolboy; no longer did I conduct an extravagant weekly correspondence with a similarly struck cousin of mine, in which we put the Surrey eleven through a fantastic set of picaresque

Rabelaisian adventures because they inspired our childish humour and we loved them so. By this time I had spread my interests; earning a living, studying, marrying, begetting and becoming aware of such besetting topics as literature, the arts, the law and the menace of nationalism diluted in the thirties my insensate concentration on the Surrey team. I was obliged to curtail my hours at the Oval, though in spirit I was with them as I had always been. Keen Surrey supporter as I was, I specialized less from that time on; I reached the stage quite early when provided there was good cricket a Surrey defeat concerned me little. Added to this there was a spice lacking in their cricket. Right up to the war the Surrey I cherished was still the Surrey of the late twenties. Most aptly I recalled a poem published in 1773 by the Rev. John Dunscombe, entitled *Surrey Triumphant: the Kentishmen's Defeat*. This prophetic title embraced my most wishful thoughts of those two decades of my nonage, summed neatly up the quintessential match that I have just re-savoured in my memory, and gave me for years what seemed likely to be my nearest approach to the sweets of true success for a team too unequal and uneven to command the heights. In my mind Surrey remained triumphant, the paladins of my youth and freshness; but triumphant in imagination merely.

As we all know, there came a time, years later, after the game had got well restarted after the Second War, when Surrey at last achieved their triumph, gave back to their weary but faithful supporters the reward of a solid generation of waiting. In 1950 they shared the championship with Lancashire; good indeed, it was an honour and a pleasure, but we were not satisfied, we wanted top honours alone; and two years later the vivacious Stuart Surridge led them to the top against all comers, crowned and sealed the patient team-building of several seasons with victory after resounding victory, and for the first time since the First World War the championship took up its home at the Oval. They might well rejoice, for it was a destroying combination that they had assembled in their chocolate caps. And now mark the curious paradox: the pride of Surrey in the twenties, my Surrey, that county of genius and adventure, was in the crushing phalanx of batsmen with hardly a bowler worthy of the name to battle by their side. Now after the Second War came the turn-about; Surrey blasted their way to the top, and defied every challenge, by virtue of the most destructive bowling combination in the land; and when they went on in the next year to hold the title for the second time, less convincingly but still decisively, it was the bowlers again that carried them like a succession of great waves to their objective, in spite of, I repeat in spite of, certain weaknesses in the batting which in the days of their older fame had been their conspicuous boast. The character of the wicket had changed: from a batsman's paradise it had become the spin bowler's delight, and in the ultimate happy triumph of Surrey (in which who took deeper pleasure than I?) it was the bowlers, not the batsmen, who took the leading parts. Read over their names and remember: Alec Bedser, the finest medium-pace bowler in the world if Bradman is to be believed, carrying his big frame lightly, infinitely hostile, virtually uncollarable, difficult to play on a plumb wicket, a raging and unspeakable devil (as the Australians know) on a wet one; Jim Laker, upright, handsome, straight-backed, rasping his off-spinners from an awkward height with great strength of finger, praying all the time for a worn pitch and rejoicing in it when he got one; Tony Lock, lowering, mercurial, temperamental, digging in his quicker left-hand slows on an impeccable length, gesticulating and gyrating at every momentary twitch and turn of the game, the greatest fielder I have ever seen wear the Surrey cap—all these backed up by the fresh energetic enthusiasm of Surridge and the new lithe youngster Loader, with Clark and Eric Bedser with their off-breaks in reserve and MacMahon to understudy Lock if necessary—where in the country was a collection of bowlers to match it? The wheel had certainly turned.

Not that I would malign the batting. May has the quality of my great Surrey batsmen of the twenties, and there are commendable soundnesses in Constable, Clark, Fletcher and the like, enlivened in Fletcher (who comes from my own club) by hints of dazzle and glint that are not often enough displayed. McIntyre's cover drive, the remains of a once sparkling batsman, is nearly the finest thing to be seen when Surrey are at the wicket, and when they field he is as neat and alert behind the stumps as Strudwick or Brooks at their best. But it was the bowlers, and no one can deny it to them, who conducted Surrey to their reward, and these same bowlers, on this same ground, before this same crowd, were the chief means by which, in August 1953, England gathered the Ashes into her keeping.

Surrey triumphant; I should be content, and I am. In the scoring box sits Strudwick, in the players' dressing-room is the head coach Sandham, from the pavilion Percy Fender and Sir Jack Hobbs can watch their successors play. They are contented enough, I am certain. The great pennant floats from the flagstaff, the great ground is packed and eager, the great county has deserved well of its followers. Yet when the bell rings from the pavilion and the umpires come out and Surrey's opponents take the field—in the momentary hush I find myself wishing (and Surridge and his men will know I mean them no disrespect whatever) that out of that white gate, with a proud glance at the flag they never knew, could come Hobbs and Sandham once more, with the shining-haired Ducat and solid Tom Shepherd to follow, and Peach and the guileful Fender to reap the full rewards of character and genius— men great in their generation, who were denied through no fault of their own the honour that (forgive me) lesser men than they have been able to achieve.

CHAPTER FIVE

PAVILIONED IN SPLENDOUR

AGAINST that necessary background; against the ever-present ritual, the personal keenness, the schoolboyish pursuit of the game itself and our curious private substitute for it; against the local accident of our Surrey loyalty and against the historical vicissitudes of first-class cricket in the middle and late twenties; against that necessary background Victor and I came slowly to the threshold of adult manhood. I do not contend that this affected in any way our sense of social responsibility or our intellectual development; I hope it did; but I am bound to confess that on looking contemplatively back I do not find a great deal of evidence for it. However, this book is not a spiritual or intellectual autobiography, but one man's record of a lifetime's fascinated interest in a single rather complex activity; and in the context of that activity alone, we found by the time we arrived at the mature age of sixteen or so that we were beginning not only to know what we liked but also very positively to know what we didn't like, and among the items listed in the second category was sitting in the shilling seats at the Oval.

It might have been different had we lived closer to Lord's, where conditions for the unprivileged are so very much more comfortable than they are in the concrete austerity of its ugly sister.* But we didn't live closer to Lord's, and altogether saw comparatively little of that great ground, though we made a ritual point of attending the Middlesex and Sussex match at Whitsun, usually on the third day, when there was often a considerable finish. No, we were conditioned to spectatorship among the blown dust and orange peel of the inhospitable Kennington benches. There was no shelter when it rained and no shelter when it shone; it was impossible to attain a vantage point from which you could see, as it were, down into the

* I speak, of course, of 1927. *Nous avons*, I am glad to report, *changé tout cela.*

field of play as distinct from across it (much less get behind the bowler without paying extra to sit in the Vauxhall stand, where you were so far away from the game that you might just as well have been in Vauxhall Station); your view was consequently *across* the field, and you saw the ball move dizzyingly before a confusing backcloth of spectators' faces and bodies and legs on the other side of the ground. This would result before the day's play was half over in the beginnings of a headache or a series of exasperating moves to find more advantageous positions. The situation deteriorated so badly that we at last began to direct the envious eyes, which we had for some time been casting on the great tiered pavilion that over-hung us all, towards the more practical question of the immediate main chance; and in 1928, early spring, we persuaded our several parents to indulge us to the extent of schoolboy membership of the county club.

We were enrolled as members as early as the February; and words cannot express the pitch of anticipatory excitement to which the imminence of the new season was to bring us. In addition to the obvious luxury in which we were henceforth destined to enjoy the spectacle of our first-class matches, we had the prized privilege, which we were not going to be behind-hand in exercising at the earliest possible instant, of practising under the eyes of county coaches on the holy turf itself. Half-way through April the school-boy members were invited to avail themselves of this scheme; and alternating arrangements for practice at school (which also took place for the favoured few in the school holidays) with carefully spaced dates at the Oval, we organized our pre-season cricket into a very tidy and attractive pattern long before the tiresome spring term was over and the sports and other irrelevances out of the way. Thus it was that I entered the Oval pavilion as a player before ever I occupied it as a spectator; that is, if I may stretch a point. I suppose I may be allowed without taint of *suggestio falsi* to count my advance from the pavilion in flannels, carrying bat and pads, as a prelude to functioning on the Oval as a player; but that is about all I have to boast of. In actual fact my début in the pavilion cost me (as my débuts everywhere tend to do) a wealth of humiliation that took a considerable time to pay off; for arriving late and alone, and mistak-ing a hurried direction, I began to change on my own in the wrong dressing-room, surprised at the lack of company but too scared to embark on any further foraging trips; and being discovered by some official or other when half-dressed was bundled with an armful of hastily snatched-up gear into a dressing-room full of my curious and watchful contemporaries. That I have since found reason to believe that the room into which I was thus pitchforked is the historic chamber where England elevens assemble for Test matches is no consolation at all. It took me two or three sessions at the nets to recover from the prickly heat.

The practice was in the hands of a mild-mannered and tentative retired Army officer named Major Luther, tall and willowy with a shock of grey hair on a handsome head that swayed engagingly as he walked. Under his direction, and no doubt concentrating upon taking a rise out of him whenever possible, was a posse of junior professionals, among whom Bob Gregory was by far the most active and encouraging. He would dart down the pitch to demonstrate a stroke, fly back to the wicket and bowl up a suitable ball—and as soon as you had despatched it into the net with what had seemed to your innocence a reasonably satisfactory wallop " Look at that TOE! " he would yell, capering frantically in three directions at once and rushing upon you, tearing at his scanty hair in eagerness to begin the demonstration all over again. Around him his dutiful colleagues wheeled up their routine deliveries. I found some of them painfully fast, notably those of a certain Lock, now the admirable groundsman who has given the Oval wicket its new and characteristic bite; and I later felt more than ever ineffective and insignificant when I came to see these terrifying bowlers in a real match and observed from the shelter of the pavilion how slow and innocuous they seemed. At the nets they were polite but perfunctory; regarded no doubt the whole business as a depressing chore (to this the ebullient Gregory appeared to be an exception); and made occasional shadowy gestures with their hands and arms to show you how you should have played the last one that bowled you, without (and this always excepts Gregory) translating their commentaries into intelligent speech. Half in and half out of the picture pottered the amiable Luther, in flannels and a curious long white overcoat, hugging the book with the elaborate time-tabled entries regulating our schedule of innings. Part clerk, part player, part organizer,

Right: DENIS COMPTON,
IN HIS FIRST SEASON,
COMING OUT TO BAT
AT THE OVAL WITH
PATSY HENDREN. (*p.* 130)

Below: DENIS COMPTON BATTING AGAINST AUSTRALIA, 1948.

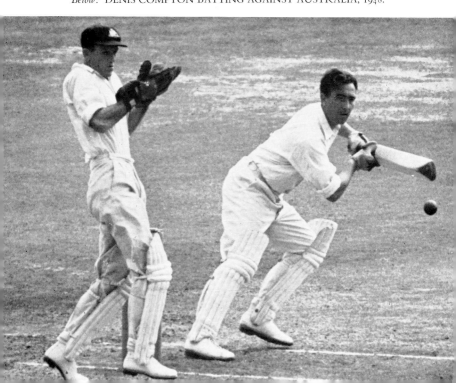

Right: REG FLAVELL
AND RONALD MASON
(THE AUTHOR)
OPENING THE INNINGS
FOR BANSTEAD
SECOND ELEVEN. (*p.* 157)

Below: BANSTEAD CRICKET GROUND. (*p.* 141)

part waif and stray, the good man threaded his way through these
manœuvres without ever seeming to have full control. Once in a
while he would bowl, a nice ballooning half-volley as often as not;
once he batted for a spell with two or three professionals whacking
down all they had at him. I cannot remember how he shaped;
to do him justice, I think he had been not so long before a creditable
cricketer enough at the Minor County level; and his batting so far as
I remember it showed traces of quality and style. We boys laughed
ribaldly at him behind his long swaying back; to us he was just
another raggable schoolmaster, not a middle-aged man selflessly
giving up his time (whether he was doing this for love I do not
know) to organizing for a parcel of boys a pleasure and a privilege
that they would never entirely forget.

It was an attractive, exciting time. Some of the genuine first team
men would occasionally appear, and we would rub shoulders
breathlessly with Barling or Garland-Wells. Brooks, the new
wicket-keeper, kept in a net one day; another day Fender came, a
long beaky figure in mufti, meeting his professionals for the first
time that season with friendly and welcoming handshakes. " Hello,
Tom, how are you? Ah, Bob, nice to see you, how are you keeping? Yes, very well, thanks, very well indeed "—and so on all round
the affable circle. And across the middle the mowers and the hoses
were out, and one of the scoreboards was being painted, and men
were astride the awnings on the pavilion roping the canvas—all the
buzzing preparations for another summer, in which we, we felt,
were to participate, in our access of privilege, in closer proximity
to the fountain-head than ever before. Standing on the balcony
in our shirts—that same balcony from which just over a quarter of a
century later Hutton waved acknowledgments to the crowd that
surged at his feet when the Ashes had at last been regained—we
could look down to where the glorious springtime greenness flowed
away from under us to wash against the far confines of the Vauxhall
stand. A dressing-room full of boys behind us, an empty pavilion
about us, a great space of green with a flurry of busy activity in the
corner by the scoreboard under the gasometer; the eye could take
all this serenely in and travel up the road with the clanging trams
to the dim arch where the main line runs through Vauxhall Station,
away beyond the housetops to the gulls above the river, and

6—BP

overlooking us all, to the left of the gasworks, the Victoria Tower with the flag flying over it, and Baldwin and MacDonald and Lloyd George below.

The pavilion itself yielded up its treasures more slowly. It came to life more readily when the season opened and its members began to fill it, when cricketers at stated intervals went in and out of it and the tobacco smoke rose around and above it in hanging pervasive clouds of blue. At practice time it seemed an echoing shell, expectant of occupants perhaps, but for all that unreal; but on the day of the first game it acquired an organic life and purpose, and we annexed it for our own on that day in a sense in which we had not found it possible to do so before. The first game was a trial game (my life's climacterics seem to hinge themselves on Surrey trials), the earliest and lesser of the two that Surrey laid on before the season began. What notice they took of the form there displayed I do not know; the earlier gave to the unfledged colts, both professional and amateur, a chance to loosen their shoulders and partake at least of the illusion of a match; while the later of the two deployed the whole strength of Surrey, Hobbs, Sandham, Fender and all, together with the most promising of the juniors.

Perfunctory and unimportant as the play was bound to be, it was our first taste of cricket seen from the Oval pavilion, and bright and early on the first day of all we arrived with our sandwiches for a full-day session as keyed up and critical as if it had been a Test match. I am not going to recite in order the details of the day (historically it may be said to be of interest as the first appearance on the Oval of an England fast bowler, Alf Gover); it was chilly and dull throughout, and our emotions were concentrated mainly upon the spectacle of the good Luther captaining one of the sides with all his vague courtesy and amiability. In the second over of the game he put a dolly catch on the floor at slip, scrabbling at it as it dropped with a frantic despair which gave us inexpressible joy and contentment; and when later in the day he went in to bat, and in the course of a gallant little innings of something over a dozen he slid for five or six yards on his bottom when going for a quickish single, we reverted to despicable type and were once again the snotty little boys hugely amused over the physical discomfiture of an elder and better.

But the day remains memorable less for the cricket than for our first entranced exploration of the pavilion itself, storey upon dark storey of hushed corridors and great landings opening out into wide and lofty rooms, bars, dressing-rooms, offices, reading-rooms, writing-rooms and the Lord knows what beside. Every room and every corridor was hung with paintings, prints, photographs, posters, of every conceivable quality and size. A vast photograph of W. G. Grace, a beautiful action snap of Hobbs jumping out to drive, an elaborate painting of one W. E. Roller going in to bat in the year 1886, vied for impressiveness with an execrable delineation of the entire membership and staff of the Surrey County Cricket Club in 1910, depicted as standing in and around and in front of the pavilion and embellished with a key diagram indicating the identity of every single member of this very considerable crowd. Up and down the walls were innumerable score cards of historic matches— the Triangular Tests, the match in which Victoria* scored 1,107, the match in which Hobbs equalled and beat W. G.'s record number of centuries—printed on silk and framed. We gazed at these treasures for hours, gazed at the photographs of the Australian eleven of 1905, of the Gentlemen's eleven of 1911, of Lord Hawke and Lord Harris, of Digby Jephson and Morice Bird, of Lillywhite and Wisden and Caffyn and Alfred Mynn. A plethora assailed us and we tottered about during the intervals in a quiet stupor; we read every paper in the reading-room; we wrote letters on the notepaper most bounteously provided in the writing-room. In the long central chamber, corresponding to the Long Room at Lord's, we stood awestruck before the beautifully designed board showing the state of the matches simultaneously playing up and down the country; down in the basement we contemplated, with an even more dizzy-ing sense of the wonders of applied science, the busy little tape-machine which fed it. (In our maturer wisdom we tumbled to it that this little device was cherished by the membership and staff, not only for the readiness of its cricket information, but for the racing results as well. I have seen a batsman walk straight off the illustrious Oval amid the applause of the congregated crowd, and walk straight down into the basement without separating himself from his cap, bat, pads or gloves, to satisfy himself at the very earliest possible instant of time of the result of the 3.30.)

* The State, not the Queen.

What with finding the best vantage points for watching, and making ourselves acquainted with every available nook and cranny in the place from the clock under the flagstaff to the basement bar, and incidentally noting for future reference all those points in the game which we considered the finer, and they were legion, our first day in that pavilion passed like a fleeting dream. I remember I wrote at least two letters on club notepaper in the intervals of all my other activities; and Victor was button-holed, not for the last time either, by an elderly member who qualified in our minds as Crackpot Member Number One. As this match was a mere perfunctory trial, the attendance was naturally slender, though I dare say there were several hundred old buffers there all told; and it was not long, in terms of weeks and months, before we began to know a number of these characters very well indeed by sight. Some of them to our certain knowledge came every day there was a match on, and for all I know when there wasn't (one or two of them contrived to convey the impression that they would hardly have noticed the difference). Most of these familiar frequenters were hale, snuffy, genial old men in their sixties and seventies, taking retirement very easily indeed and using it in a way I still have half a mind to emulate myself, when my time comes; and they sat and gossiped in their worn tweeds, bringing out their sandwich tins and their lemonade bottles at the intervals, their old brown hands manipulating the field-glasses with the teased leather straps—patently enjoying the endless variations of this game they could no longer play. A quiet, inoffensive, slightly cracked company, they came and went, a sober background to our *naïveté* and enthusiasm; and so familiar did they become to us as part of the furniture of the place that it comes as quite a shock to me now— did, in fact, two minutes ago, as I was writing this very paragraph— to realise that, as this time I speak of was well over twenty-five years ago, it is very probable that they are all dead. The pavilion and the pictures are there; the game proceeds on the everlasting green before them; but the background members have imperceptibly changed.

They were there in force on our first day, however, or at least the solid nucleus was there, to build themselves all unconsciously into our minds. Three characters were to impress themselves particularly on our dual consciousness during the three seasons or so while we served our fascinating apprenticeship before becoming blasé full members with the privilege of introducing Tom, Dick and Harry— three characters who, I regret to say, rendered their images indelible with me by reason of their several infirmities. One was a large heavy man, not by pavilion standards very old (probably in his late fifties or early sixties) who for some unhappy reason carried his great head perpetually on one side, projected forward as if he had his chin painfully impaled on a spike. He had a gloomy, contemplative expression, as well might be worn by one in that awkward situation, and was frequently to be observed making one of a small group at the bar in earnest discussion of some imponderable problem, holding his head judicially poised, as always, and carrying in his hand a glass of something short. My memories of him are utterly passive and static, a ruminant figure of an appealing and melancholy fascination; whereas the second of the three, even more pitifully visited by infirmity, provided an active contrast to the first brooding Titan. This man was small, birdlike, eager, and incurably palsied. He trembled intensely and constantly; he smoked a pipe and it beat a fierce tattoo on his teeth as he removed or replaced it; yet he was cheerful, interested, assiduous in following the cricket both at the Oval before him and on the bulletin board; and never far from friends with whom he engaged in gusty discussions. The third, most portentous of all, was the public Crackpot Number One to whom I have already alluded. A tall rangy man with a ginger beard and an eye of an Old Testament prophet, he prowled ominously among the spectators seeking whom he might devour. He cornered Victor in the reading-room on the first day, and I, hovering on the outskirts, came in for most of it. Some time later he cornered me, this time in the lavatory, and I had it all over again. His theme was mystifying and apparently quite irrelevant; I do not understand it and I doubt if I ever shall; but at some time in his life he had conceived an unbounded admiration for the skill at amateur soccer of the celebrated brothers A. M. and P. M. Walters, famous figures in the game in, I should say, about 1890; and solemnly in 1928 in a pavilion dedicated to a game quite other than soccer he would hold us with his glittering eye until he had delivered a short encomium on the outstanding merits of these two players. " Have you heard," he would begin in a rasping but rather compelling monotone, " about the brothers Walters? " On that day neither Victor nor I could have distinguished them, even if given the option, from the brothers Karamazov; and our momentary silence was sufficient to provide his cue. He went on purposefully with this extraordinary eulogy, for perhaps a minute or more; then he concluded, in a tone of real and rather touching reverence—" Yes. The brothers Walters. A. M. and P. M. Walters "—and his voice died a little breathlessly from what I am convinced was a genuine and moving pride for a greatness that he had glimpsed once and which perhaps had so overwhelmed the delicate balance of his mind in the past as to help it to this pathetic derangement. " Yes, the brothers Walters," he sighed on a dying fall, and moved sadly away. We were amused and interested rather than scared; and several times in the succeeding years I would hear that voice accosting, whenever and wherever the fancy took it, some surprised fellow member with this urgent message that plagued its bearer so often to the recital as if it were calling, appealing, tremulously across an immense void, " Have you heard, did you ever hear, you, sir, or you, sir, or you; Oh please listen, for this is urgent life-and-death news I bring you, news of a beauty and a grace I once saw and am compelled to pass on, and am content to do so, until I die—have you heard, you, sir, or you, sir, or you, about the brothers Walters? "

He can hardly be living still, this tormented single-minded soul; I hope that in the engulfing kindness of death the furies have left him to rest not too far from his heroes; they were kindly men (who gave up the game they loved for the sake of their parents' peace of mind when their brother died of a football injury) and surely they will receive him with understanding and mete him his appropriate reward. And if the palsied enthusiast is at last serene and unmoving, and the sad contemplative man is straightened to an undistorted serenity, then I am more content with death's ravages than I can be, in the region of this game, with most of its cruel severity. Cricket must have lightened, for them, sufferings and sorrows at which I would not presume to guess; in their turn their presence gave colour and depth to a boy's ripening experience of life. They will hardly grudge me the value of that experience which they helped to enlarge.

But our greatest luxury was reserved for the evening, when play had closed and the stairways were crowded and the cars hooted and the newsboys cried at the entrances. With an ironic eye for the hot and dusty crowds shuffling with their empty rucksacks and their crumpled mackintoshes to the exits and the bus queues, we went leisurely downstairs to the superbly appointed lavatories, and scrubbed ourselves rosy amid steaming basinfuls of gorgeously hot water. Towels, hairbrushes, combs, and all the ultimate decent needs of a refined civilization were laid on with a bounty before which we could only gasp. We never actually had baths there, but I have no doubt that we could have done so if we had wanted to. As it was we rioted and splashed in sybaritic contentment, flinging towels with gay extravagance into the waste baskets provided for the purpose though we had barely touched them with wet fingers. Half an hour after the οἱ πολλοι had scuffled and jostled themselves sweatily to the gates, we would emerge from the lower regions in a state of spiritual pride and complacency that can hardly be divined by one who has not had the experience for himself, washed, brushed, combed to an unnatural glossy Sutcliffe-like brightness, reeking to high heaven of several different kinds of soap, and invaded by an unconquerable sense of physical well-being that had already (the time was about seven o'clock) begun to cry in our depths for food. On the way out (this is now, of course, to speak of matches later in the season than our first memorable trial run) we would study the bulletin board; we would gaze excitedly at some of the players as, changed and burnished like ourselves, they would stroll through to the exits (the time when Garland-Wells, who had impeccably dressed himself in his gents' summer suiting under the impression that he would be needed no more that day, had to resume his flannels in full view of our delighted Paul Pry selves to go out and field for one over, is in this story but not of it; let us draw a veil.) Then, satiated with the day's wonders, we would go home to supper; and as like as not career off on our bicycles five minutes after to the recreation ground for an hour's intense cricket before dark.

They were days, it is unnecessary to repeat, that are unrecapturable in their freshness and their irresistible charm. The world was all before us, as before Adam and Eve, and we had not been cast out

of Eden, but admitted into a pleasance in exchange for which, as
far as we were concerned, Eden could have been yours for the asking
and a bag of sweets thrown in. Pretentious as it sounds, we had
entered into a new possession; an experience which in this rapacious
and imperfect world can be as precious, if rightly savoured, as any
in our lives. Few who have not shared the feeling can focus in the
imagination even the half of the image of the reality; of a morning,
say, in August, with school and exams over and the holidays stretch-
ing into the illimitable inane before us, eleven o'clock and the
ground filling, the careful business of seat selection complete,
whether on the single-row balcony or high under the clock or for a
change on the left in that part of the pavilion to which ladies were
grudgingly admitted; the trams dundering by outside the fence, a
train whistle from the shunting yards near Waterloo Station;
the sky bright blue over the Kennington slates, deeper and hazier
above the Gothic stone of Westminster, and the air fresher than
you could think it possible, creamy with the promise of full high
noon, flavoured now and then with a waft from the brewery
hardly maltier than the smell of new bread; the droning hoot of a
tug making Vauxhall Bridge on the high tide; and Victor returning
from some sortie or forage far down in the pavilion's bowels—
" Here you are—bit of chocolate and two pieces of cake. There's a
crowd round the notice board, the team's up for the Middlesex
match. I didn't stop to look. Just passed Fender on the landing,
looks as if he had a thick night last night. Here, move over, I can't
see from here. There's a chap smoking in the non-smoking seats.
Oh, and the Shaky Man's downstairs, been lighting his pipe since
half-past ten. And I saw X again, in a bow tie, he looks awful.
Don't eat all that chocolate now, there won't be any left for lunch.
Oh yes, and I've seen the Brothers Walters."

It was at this promising stage in our careers that we embarked
together upon a joint enterprise that may be said to be enjoying its
remoter repercussions to this very day. I have already told of our
more youthful adventures in literary creation, in which we elabor-
ated in high mouth-filling journalese the tales of our fictitious
matches and tours. These we had continued almost up to the time
when we became members of the Surrey Club; but the transition

in our status marked also an alteration in the nature of our medium of expression, and as soon as we took up our new privileges we determined to signalize our promotion in a new way. We would write an account, full and detailed and personal, keeping as far off conventional journalese as possible, of every first-class cricket match we attended. To this end we purchased a stout exercise book and a small notebook; armed with the notebook we attended the matches, jotting down scores, bowling changes, climatic *bouleversements,* philosophic comments, humorous drawings and anything else that took our fancy; and from this conglomerate hodge-podge we solemnly wrote up our accounts in the stout exercise book in what we fondly imagined to be our most mature literary style. (Who was expected to read these productions is not clear; but we read them ourselves with cooings of delighted satisfaction; and I cannot help confessing that when the other day I came across one of these volumes it brought back with a real authenticity the atmosphere of the match whose description I read so many years after.)

It still bothers me how we had time to spare, not only from our more legitimate activities, but from all our other exertions ancillary to cricket. Apart from all the harlequinades that I have already described so exhaustingly, we each kept voluminous scrapbooks into which we pasted every single picture of cricket or cricketers that any paper we happened to get ever printed, together with numerous scores and columns of comment. Victor, whose parents seemed to take in every paper published, amassed a vast collection of these scrapbooks that were our everlasting delight to re-read; I, who was furnished with one morning paper and one evening paper only, lagged far in the rear, though Victor generously aided me with duplicates. Yet backward as I was I still have five bursting volumes, records of nearly three unremitting years. Why I gave up, as I did, bang in the middle of the Australian tour of 1930, would be a cricket mystery were it not that I think that for once, in that year, Latin, Greek and English Literatures had to take precedence.

But the cuttings were a sideline. In 1928 the reportage was the thing, and in that trial match of that year, when we first sat in the pavilion at the Oval, the notebook came for the first time into assiduous play. I wish it were extant now—or do I? The living witness of at least one of the finished volumes is a crying advertisement of schoolboy portentousness, precocious self-consciousness and flamboyant exhibitionism; which is to say, writing that turns the milk sour. It is interesting at this stage to compare and contrast the literary styles of the collaborators; Victor, who read widely and voraciously in newspapers, affected a slick journalistic streamline (" Constantine managed to get a four in edgeways—Tyldesley's foot was not in the right place"), while I for my part, being a fancied man in English composition who preened himself on the quiet for having read a couple of books by Thackeray, would go in for " literary " turns of phrase of carefully minted quality (" The slips and the wicket-keeper sprang galvanized into life, and a baying roar of ' Haraat? ' swept across the field. The umpire's hand went up "). Common to both contributors was a sorry propensity to cliché (" the Marlborough boy," " the Indian Prince," " swept it like a flash," " a minor tragedy," are random anthology-pieces that I have picked up in a couple of minutes, and I have no doubt that a careful search, for which at present I have not the stomach, would reveal a very large number of such). The only quality that distinguished these lucubrations from the most inexpert scribbles in the least satisfactory of newspapers was a ribald vein of libellous comment of which, much to my regret, I am still, even at this distance of time, inhibited by decorum and prohibited by law from giving effective examples. The reference to X in my report of Victor's conversation a page or so back is nothing to the proliferation of rudeness that accrued to our descriptions of any player to whom we might for the slenderest reason, or indeed for no reason at all, have taken a dislike. These remarks varied from succinct ones such as " Several of the Notts team were seen arriving; all looked at least moderately respectable. Blank was also seen. He did not," to elaborate and unfounded allegations against respectable public figures of drunkenness, bribery and corruption, and general looseness of morals. I can only say that in calm retrospect this aspect of our literary output reads deplorably; it is only to be excused on the grounds that in our then exalted and unstable condition of excitement we thought it funny, and in the retarded state of our literary development we felt it worth committing to paper. It was naturally neither.

Nevertheless, I feel that this grotesque activity was not entirely without value. We began it in the spring of 1928 and it dried up, again without apparent reason, in the middle of the report of the Champion County match of 1929—two crowded seasons of delight and alert assimilation of new familiarities and new communities. Then, as with the scrapbooks and the roulette cricket, other pre-occupations encroached, and quite naturally and unobtrusively we dropped them. I was battling severely with Greek and Latin, Victor with modern languages; the urgencies of our own personal cricket, of which I have already written, occupied us in the summer, the sterner realities of study in the winter. For my part I had begun to read widely and indiscriminately; Victor, for his, had ventured on an acquaintance with great music that has ripened into a familiarity and a love that has been with him ever since. Sanity was returning, kindly and unfussily replacing the temporary distractions of mono-mania. Yet, as I say, it had not been valueless. It had helped, just as our otherwise worthless school essays had helped, in the marshal-ling and the expression of our ideas not only about cricket but about any topic we were called upon to discuss ; and in the particular field of cricket it had performed the highly important service of infusing character and drama, however crude, into our view of a game which certainly contains these elements in plenty but so often in discussion and description finds itself stripped bare of them. I have never enjoyed the bare statistics of the business; much less since I learned, in company with Victor in our scrappy and juvenile essays in impromptu amateur journalism, that unless this game is coloured with humour and humanity and the life of the mind it will deteriorate into a statistician's Tom Tiddler's Ground whose gold and silver will on analysis be so much dust and ashes. I can pardon myself for those early excesses; for I feel them to have been sympto-matic of an instinctive understanding that added itself to the other accrued scraps of education that cricket was putting in my way, and of which the previous chapters have been designed as the cumulative record.

CHAPTER SIX

THE MASTER

THE cult of the hero is discredited in these disillusioned days, and there is ample warrant for it. There is a point, as we have discovered in the past generation, where a healthy romanticism runs riot and goes rotten, its objectives distorted and its idealisms warped. Emotionalism, we conclude, is not to be trusted; the hero, an age-old projection of a subjective emotionalism, part father, part god, part wishful image of the self, blossomed in the nineteenth century first in Napoleonic and then in Bismarckian disguise, to ripen horribly in the twentieth in manifestations which in immediacy and in aftermath are bedevilling us to this day. The hero is either a fraud or a madman; Steerforth seduces little Em'ly and Stanhope goes on the bottle, Napoleon goes to St. Helena by way of Waterloo and Hitler goes to the bunker by way of universal destruction. Misplaced weakness or misplaced strength, it is all much the same, it is merely a question of the relative coefficient of destructiveness. Destroy an illusion or destroy a world; it is the hero's prerogative to do one or the other; in extreme cases, both.

The cricketer's heroes have their destructiveness mercifully extracted at the start, because however powerful their fascination for him they do not invade the private province of his moral sense. We like to think that cricket is not an immoral game, and it is not; many like, moreover, to think that it is positively moral, which in most senses it is not either. To label it amoral appears to credit it with a kind of Machiavellian or Voltairean swagger that is not at all characteristic of it; but that is what it is. In spite of strenuous endeavours by certain men of good will, it preserves a detachment from the intricacies of moral debate that is necessary to its existence as an independent recreation. The cricketer hero makes no demands on his worshipper's conscience or his worshipper's loyalty. He merely, by performing so transcendently better than his worshipper would ever be able to do himself, becomes identified in the worshipper's mind with the heights of his own aspirations. If, in addition to extreme ability in performance, he happens to possess an attractive public personality, his hold on his devotees will be unbelievably stronger. Jack Hobbs and Denis Compton are examples of this fortunate blend of the clever and the good; they are members of a little band of heroes who, I think, are led pre-eminently and unchallengeably by the almost legendary Victor Trumper, a player whose shining brilliance and resource seem to have been matched by an altogether unusual personal sweetness of character. Yet even these public paragons ask nothing from us. They are here for our delight, that is all. Their virtues are happy incidentals, not essential to their skill, which is what has entrapped our concentrated attention.

In writing, in this chapter and the next, on two great cricketers who have in turn filled for me the necessary rôle of hero, I shall be aware all the time that I am dealing now with what is in essence common property. Hobbs was my hero in the twenties, but he was the hero of I do not know how many thousand other boys (and men too) at the same time. Therefore what I have to say about him is by no means, you will think, original or unique. There is no point in my outlining for you the very familiar tale of his career and his records, even of his well-known days of particular success, for Surrey or for England; the reference books have repeated all these facts until they are dizzy. And, as I said, there is nothing in the slightest degree unusual (in fact it is rather commonplace) in having been a Hobbs-worshipper. But because I have set myself the task of examining one man's, my own, attitude to the game in enough detail to make the study of possible use to anyone trying to come to closer terms with the game's peculiar fascination, I am bound to dilate at some length on this essential relationship between devotee and hero which has existed, and will go on existing, as long as the game itself. And no book that I were to write on cricket, with whatever real or pretended purpose, could be complete without a recognition, in some form or another, of the supremacy of Jack Hobbs in my day and generation. I am trying, in writing of Hobbs and of Hammond, to record nothing about these men that did not have an actual effect, emotional or otherwise, on me. I am examining them now as part of my approach to the game, not as historical elements in its formal story. They are of course conspicuous in that context; but as for that and all that they did, is it not written in the Book of Wisden?

I was born and bred, as I have already explained, a Surrey man; and from the moment when I became aware of it as an independent county Jack Hobbs' name stood at the head of it, its supreme representative. Groping back in my memory I cannot at all recall the first time I heard his name; he was *there*, in my consciousness, enthroned, before I ever had time or leisure to inquire why. In Surrey the name of Hobbs was paramount and sacred; from Vauxhall Bridge to Coldharbour he was undisputed king. Before I had ever set eyes on him he was the cricketer with whom I most felt, in some sort, an emotional identification. I rejoiced with his successes, and they were mercifully regular: I desponded with his failures, and I did not need, as may be gathered, to despond very often. It is fair enough evidence of the curious hypnotism that attracted me willy-nilly into this relationship that I followed him as it were entirely on trust for an inordinate length of time; for he became thus mysteriously established as my own property midway through the 1920 season, and I am compelled solemnly to put my hand on my heart and swear that it was 1927 before I ever saw him make a century. For years I trailed hopefully after him, still nursing the unconquerable hope. I have already recorded that he absented himself altogether from the first match I ever watched; and that in the second, two years later, he failed me with the whole day before him to fulfil himself in my eyes. In the next year, in the Lord's Test match against South Africa, he made over 200 the day after I attended; in the Champion County match at the end of that season he was out last thing on the evening before I had planned to be there. In an intermediate county match where I did see him bat, he prodded an innocuous ball on to his wicket when he had made 10; in another big match, the next season, I saw him field on the day after he had made 106. On a rainy Monday in August 1925 when the world hung breathless on the anticipation of his equalling Grace's record of centuries, and when for the time being nothing would go right for him, I watched him come out to bat with

Sandham against Middlesex with a day and a half to spare and a near-hysterical Oval crowd to back him to the last run; when he had scored 4 rain stopped play not only for the day but for the match. In the corresponding game in the next season he was in the field all the first day when my parents allowed me to go, and made 176 not out on the second, when I was obliged to escort an uncle to the Zoo; in the Test match at Lord's against Australia he once again made his century after a day when I had watched him field. On one other occasion I arrived at lunch-time when he had made 57, and he got out before he had added more than a dozen to his score; in two other innings he arrived in the region of the twenties and was then caught, once by Hubble, once by the looming Barratt of Notts. In between and around these deplorable occasions the newspapers showed him as having achieved fantastic and nigh unbelievable records, which for all the evidence I have ever been shown in their support might have been attained like my own on a roulette wheel. In England and Australia, for his county and for his country, Jack Hobbs piled Pelion upon Ossa in records and in runs during those six or seven seasons of my most enthusiastic studentship; and I was never there.

He made glorious amends one morning in 1927, when an uncle of mine who was a member of the Surrey Club gave me entry into the pavilion, and when almost for the first time I saw these Titans life-size; Notts were playing, with a rather less hostile attack than they could command at their best, and on a perfect wicket Hobbs scored a hundred before lunch on the opening day. I wish I could retail the beauties of that innings stroke by stroke, but the detailed recollection has faded. All that remains to me is the image of him batting there on a warm sunless August day, capless throughout, neat and unhurried and brilliant; and of the deep satisfaction that pervaded me for the rest of the day, and for long after, at having at last seen my hero to adequate measure. It was one of those Surrey days of which I have already recorded the type; more than 500 runs on the board before the end, and a genial Fender flogging a sick attack from tea to supper. For me the day remains consecrated to the hero, the first concrete evidence I had ever been offered of his legendary mastery. My loyalty was triumphantly upheld.

Not many days later I watched the New Zealanders play Surrey at the Oval—a young side with more promise than performance, not yet considered ripe for Test status but giving signs of quality in reserve, unleashed upon us years later in the persons of Donnelly and Sutcliffe. On a sweltering August day the New Zealanders stodged rather formlessly until nearly six o'clock; the Surrey attack was without Fender; the only top-class batsman that New Zealand possessed (Dempster) was out in the first ten minutes, and the day wore somewhat painfully away without character or much incident, as we shifted and writhed (for nearly the last time) on our shilling seats. Hobbs and Sandham came in for less than half an hour at the end of the day; it was not only the quality of the match that was transformed, but the quality, it seemed, of life itself. Even I, an unblushing Hobbsolater, trembled for these young and inexperienced bowlers, energetic, optimistic, gay, who in twenty-five minutes, at a period of the day when a normal opening batsman prefers to let everything alone or indeed not to go in to bat at all, were shredded systematically into flinders by this unapproachable batsman, were hung with every conceivable emblem of futility. I felt myself even then exclaiming inwardly, " They should never have been asked to do it. It wasn't *fair!* " It was an attack as gallant and useless as the charge of the Light Brigade. The half-hour lives with me as a display of ravishing brilliance so dazzling that once again the concomitant details have slipped through the gap of my memory ; all but two transcendent cracks to square leg off fast good-length balls, timed like a heavyweight's punch and signed on their way with a sprung-steel flick of the wrists as the bat swept laterally across the line of the ball. During the magical half-hour he *played* with them, treated them to all his tricks, made it supremely clear that he could do precisely what he chose with any single ball they liked to bowl him, and would at a pinch take on two at a time. At close of play his score was somewhere in the thirties or forties and Sandham's had barely arrived at ten; and next day (when of course I could not go) he completed the hundred that by the testimony of all the New Zealanders was the finest innings played against them that summer. Thus twice in one week he made up for me for the multifarious frustrations of the past. I never felt disappointed in him again.

I came upon Jack Hobbs at the height and flush of his strange

Indian Summer that has had no adequate parallel in the career of any batsman save W. G. Grace. The First World War cut his career into two disjointed blocks—ten seasons the earlier, about sixteen the later. Those who saw him before 1914 have not breath or vocabulary to describe the charm and skill of his play; from about 1909 onwards he seems by all accounts to have been the wonder of all the gay world, flawless in classical technique as he was adventurous in romantic daring. He himself has somewhere or other said with his characteristic diffidence, "I wasn't bad after the war; but you should really have seen me before it." Well, he should know; all I can say is, if his brilliance before 1914 outdazzled his brilliance after 1918, then there has been nothing in English or Australian cricket, not Woolley or McCabe or Macartney or Bradman or Hammond or Compton or Hutton at their most richly prolific moments, to come within bowing distance of what must have been a quite unusual excellence. I have seen pictures of the young Hobbs; they do not tell me much—there are none, that I know of, to equal in felicity those classic snapshots of Victor Trumper jumping out to drive, two of the finest action pictures ever taken. No, they are mostly static, a little awkward in the way that old photographs affect; showing a delicate pallid youth with a preoccupied, rather scared look out of eyes that incline to pop, under a self-conscious Surrey cap set straight on his head. A retiring young man with quiet ambitions and a hidden resolve to fulfil them; by 1914 probably the completest batsman in cricket, with a bagful of records already from home and abroad. The war came when he was thirty-one, and before cricket got properly on its legs again he was rising thirty-seven; a little late, perhaps, to fulfil more than a fraction of the promise of the prewar years? A cut of five years from the life of a cricketer of over thirty is a very crippling cut indeed. No Australian, except Bradman, could have survived it.

Then hardly had he restarted before the disastrous season of 1921 came near to finishing him off for ever. First the snapped tendon in the twopenny-halfpenny game, putting him on the shelf for weeks; then hardly back at the job before appendicitis hit him during the Third Test and laid him on his back for the rest of the season. He could not long be kept down, and he defied the gloomiest of prophets; but I think there can be little doubt that the seasons of 1922 and 1923, when as I remember his performances were modest, were seasons during which, consciously and unconsciously, his wonderful technique underwent complete reorganisation and overhaul. When at this time I came to be consistently aware of him, he had lost his boyish timidity of expression, the sun had seasoned him, the handsomer lines of a rather striking face were beginning to trace themselves; he was turned forty. And I can only express with adequacy the fallaciousness of any suggestion that he might at this stage be considered to be in the evening rather than at the noontide of his career by reminding you that at the time of which I speak he had in first-class matches only opened the innings once with Sutcliffe. The greatest opening pair in the history of first-class cricket were only just aware of each other's potentialities. Gilbert had only this moment met Sullivan, Beaumont tentatively approached Fletcher. After a career sufficient to make lasting reputations for two ordinary men, Hobbs prepared to embark on a third. As if the advent of this new and infinitely promising junior partner had awakened him to a new enjoyment of his powers, the enjoyment of the conscious expert, Hobbs flowered for half a dozen seasons into the most consistently fruitful and various batsmanship that his own generation had seen. The slightly later rise of Hammond, the altogether unpredictable career of Bradman were in due time to emulate and eclipse, on paper at least, much of his achievement. Not in quality, though; not in kind. From the time when he was forty-two until a time when he was close under the lee of fifty, Jack Hobbs performed like an adventurous boy in the early morning shine of his first hint of power. Hammond, when he emulated him, was twenty-four; Bradman, when in fact and figure he excelled him, was twenty-two; Jack Hobbs could have been their father. In a match, in which all three were playing, at the very end of this wonderful period, Bradman made over 200 and Hammond made over 60. Hobbs did less well than either, but he hit the cleanest clinker of a hook off a good-length trimmer that put both the other giants in the shade. It signed his name, as it were, for the last time, marked off the end of a prosperity without precedent. It was in these years that casually, with his native air of mild friendliness giving grace to all his destroying actions, he piled up the records that made his name familiar in every hamlet and shippen in the land. He beat Grace's record, he scored sixteen centuries in one season, he played the highest innings ever known at Lord's, he beat the record for the highest score in the Gents *v.* Players series, he took to himself partners who helped him to I do not know how many first-wicket stands of fearful magnitude, he experienced one conspicuous week in which he made five centuries with a failure (87) lodged in the middle of them; in a dozen years he made a hundred hundreds; he played a major part in winning the Ashes in 1926 and a very important part in retaining them two years later. In those six years or so he was a public figure as he had never been in his brilliant prewar years. His summer of youth entranced the addicts; his Indian Summer captivated the whole of England. A *Punch* drawing showing an elderly auntie at her knitting dumbfounding the family by asking " Who is Hobbs? " was funny at the time and, quite possibly, still is.

His was the figure you looked for when the Surrey, the Players, the England team came out on to the field; spare, slim, self-contained, he walked with that characteristic light springy step I have already noted, the direct grace of an athlete chary of wasting a single unit of muscular effort. Under the blue cap—he never while I watched wore the Surrey cap at all; most often he chose the handsome M.C.C. touring cap with the silver George and Dragon, less regularly the England blue with the lions—his tanned face with the beaky nose was puckered and alert, the eyes no longer prominent but retired into wrinkles. He had a trick in the field of fiddling with one hand at his shirt-collar; at cover point he wore, deliberately, an air of abstraction. Again and again he ran out rash batsmen by standing yards too deep and daring the inexperienced to risk his electric swoop and bullet throw. Bradman himself fell for this one; Archie Jackson, with the first ball of his only Test innings at the Oval, avoided a like fate by the two inches by which the return missed the wicket. (The fact that cover, standing deep on his heels, was forty-seven years old, may have prompted twenty-one-year-old Jackson to risk a dash; how nearly he denied himself his last long innings in Test cricket we know now; perhaps in the perspective of time Jack Hobbs may not be sorry that his throw failed.)

But my chief memory of this man cannot separate him from his full regalia of batsmanship. Here his cap, in the pre-1914 days so staidly set on his head, was cocked more often towards one eye; as his innings lengthened it would get pushed farther and farther back on his head. As he faced the bowler his left toe, symptomatic of his restless, active, attacking temper, would turn provocatively upwards; this was not pure swagger or bravado, but was part of the fluidity of his movements towards the ball; he abhorred the static stance, was one of the most mobile batsmen of all time, his feet moving as the bowler climbed into his action. He was restless at the crease without ever seeming jumpy or perturbed; between deliveries he would let his weight go back on his heels and give his bat his famous twiddle, a gesture random and instinctive enough but appropriated by him as a trade mark which when met in other players always contrives to recall him alone; and he favoured copious pitch-prodding. One of the most abiding visions of Test cricket in the twenties is of Hobbs and Sutcliffe in the middle of the pitch heads down and prodding, elaborating no doubt matters of high policy as they came momentarily together. And one other familiar gesture remains curiously his own—in the middle of a long innings he would whip his cap off and wipe the sweat from his forehead with the forearm of the same hand, all in one movement, before setting his cap back, a little farther to the crown of his head, twiddling his bat, cocking his left toe, and returning wirily to the slaughter.

In his later years they called him " the Master "; whatever that implied it was technically appropriate. On the academic correct-ness of his batting there is no need to dilate; he was as sound as Sutcliffe and as brilliant as Woolley. Every schoolboy (and there were millions of them) who chattered and shrilled ecstatically at every run their idol stole and every boundary he hit, could have modelled his every stroke on Hobbs and never had to allow for genius. His extemporizations were rarely, in his best years, endan-gered by unorthodoxy. Later, possibly under the press of ennui (I suppose even run-getting gets tedious after a time; I never found it so) his extravagances were inspired, as only the extravagances of a genius can be. Only Hobbs could (and I am convinced that only Hobbs did) leap across his wicket with both feet off the ground, to crack a Freeman googly, on the half-volley, all along the carpet to the boundary behind the square-leg umpire, from what seemed feet outside the off stump; yet he dared and did it, and plumb off the middle of the bat too. Only Hobbs would have dared, facing in a Gents *v.* Players match a rampaging G. O. Allen inclined to pitch them short, to wander in an apparently directionless manner to meet a fast long hop rearing from a spot half a foot off the wicket on the off-side; and as it sped past him to present his bat to it reflectively, delicately, so that the ball slid down it from splice to oil-hole and cleanly bisected the slips before beating third man to the boundary. I remember these eccentricities even above his more respectable excellences. Of weakness as we commonly term it my uncritical sense retains no recollection; save perhaps a recurring tendency, in the years when I remember him best, to snick the leg-spinner to the wicket-keeper. A failure in restraint rather than in judgment, for it is said that no batsman knew better than he, and knew earlier in the ball's flight, what to play and what to leave alone.

It is time to recall one of the most signal aspects of his career's triumphs: his opening partnerships. He had made two of these immortal before I was born: with Hayward for Surrey and with Rhodes for England. Of these I cannot speak. After the war he partnered Knight for a season or so (in the course of which relationship Knight was often regarded as the more brilliant; a little testimonial he must cherish, I feel), but almost immediately found in Andrew Sandham his permanent and ideal companion. This was for Surrey alone; he never opened with Sandham for England, though there were occasions when they were in the same Test side; and for a year or two there were dalliances with Rhodes and with Russell, until in the doldrum year of 1923 something suddenly clicked in someone's mind and the incomparable association with Herbert Sutcliffe began. The partnership with Sandham was naturally the more settled and regular one; it lasted longer, covered a vastly larger number of matches, and resulted in at least one colossal opening stand of over 400, as well as in something over sixty of a hundred or more. The Hobbs-Sutcliffe combination drew the fiercer limelight from its internecine contexts; but I cannot help feeling that it may have been upon the lessons and experiences of the more modest relationship that the great classic structure of the more illustrious one was built.

Of Hobbs and Sandham as opening pair no Surrey man can ever

speak dispassionately; for years they were the necessary beginning, from them all decent things sprang, without them life wore a makeshift look. Hobbs, by reason partly of a tendency to minor strains and partly (I think) of a fairly understandable knowledge of when a rest would do him good, was oftener away from the side than his partner, and Sandham on very many occasions had to do duty, as it were, for both. This he performed with exemplary thoroughness; of all the cricketers whom I have followed through their careers, I think Sandham put most of himself into the game for the least tangible recognition. It is well known that Holmes of Yorkshire was in like case; and neither of these altogether exceptional opening batsmen ever came in for his due reward. In Yorkshire, I am told, many ranked Holmes as a more accomplished batsman than Sutcliffe. I fear that I cannot round off the story by saying that there were Surrey men who preferred Sandham to Hobbs. If there were, I never met any; but that is not the point.

Sandham was the neatest player I have ever seen. Light and trim, set as it were rather low in the water, he moved with an impeccable economy of gesture both to his place in the field and his place at the wicket. He was blessed with a curiously Mongolian cast of countenance; under the shady peak of his cap his eyes hooded themselves watchfully, never blinking, always alert, a little mysterious, inscrutable. Unlike his partner, who had at rare moments a slow and rather appealing grin, Sandham was not seen to smile; it disturbed his methodical concentration. Instead he sported a thoughtful frown, preoccupied and absorbed, advertising a purposeful determination that he put resolutely into practice. He looked narrowly down the pitch at the bowler, considering carefully such alternative ways and means that presented themselves to what was manifestly an orderly and efficient mind. The result was always correct, beautifully adapted for the moment, at times evanescently lovely. He was a delicate and persuasive stylist, with an on-drive all along the carpet that matched his partner's every bit; and a late cut of a dipping kingfisher grace that his partner just did not happen to possess, or at least display, at all. Yet the frills concerned him little; he was there to do his job—to stay, to let the bowlers break their hearts on him at one end while his partner went out and broke them all over again at the other. " For God's sake let me have a go at

Jack!" an exasperated bowler is reputed to have exclaimed. "At least he gives you half a chance."

And do the job he did. The exquisite deflections, the caressed cuts and sleight-of-hand glances, the controlled leg-hits and sudden thrashing drives of totally unexpected weight and power, gave him the assessable reward for those hours of patient self-effacement while at the other end the Master played hell and damnation to all comers alike. And the irony was in this; that more often than not, far more often than not, it was the senior partner who got out first. I would not like to swear it without book, but my present impression is that counting alone the times when I saw them open for Surrey, Sandham's aggregate of runs was greater than that of Hobbs. Hobbs would get his hundred and get out, likely enough before lunch; they would be lucky if they got rid of Sandham between tea and supper. And another thing—when Hobbs got out for nothing or next to nothing, you did not as a rule see Sandham follow. Elijah as he went out tossed his mantle to Elisha; who became two men. There was a day in the thirties when an honest Leicestershire hack bowler had the supreme impertinence to dismiss Hobbs off the first ball of the match and, just to ram home his point, Squires off the second. On that day of wrath I did not arrive at the Oval until five o'clock, having routine matters of state to transact during the day. There was no need to worry; Sandham was still there, and only one more wicket had fallen.

When Hobbs was selected for England, Sandham remained behind. The only justification for this deplorable failure of equity was that in the upper reaches Hobbs was even better supported, if that were possible. Sandham gave no public sign of disapproval, even if it had been practicable or conceivable; he continued to move trimly to his place in the field, a compact little man growing thicker with the years, and to move trimly to his place at the wicket, a modest exemplar of tuned efficiency and competence. Under a just heaven it surely might have been possible to have admitted him, only once if you like but at least once, to open the innings with Hobbs for England. It would not have been a very serious let-down. He was adequate enough to make overseas tours in his own right, to open for England in minor Test series, to compile a trifling matter of 325 in one of these games in the West Indies. Since his day batsmen have opened for England, and opened more than once, who were lamp-post cricketers by the side of Sandham. He had a most honourable career and he made over a hundred centuries, and for nearly all his life, because he stood in the shadow of a genius and by his willing unselfishness helped that genius to mature, his own conspicuous merit went unrecognized. There is a photograph at the Oval that sums it well; of the reception given to Hobbs when he went in to bat for Surrey on the first occasion in which he appeared at the Oval after beating Grace's record at Taunton. The members are on their feet, laughing, cheering, clapping, hands upraised to smite the hero on the shoulder, hats are off, men excitedly peer over their colleagues' shoulders. Through it all hastens the Master, head down, smiling in a rather frightened way, acknowledging a trifle shamefacedly the clamour of their applause. He looks grateful but he looks embarrassed. Yards behind him, unwatched, unnoticed, unrecognized, unblinking, demurely fastening his batting-glove, comes the indispensable Sandham. He walks like one who knows his place; but I would rejoice to know that a stray thoughtful member or two may have spared a cheer for him. He was a great player, of that kind of greatness which the headlines do not patronize.

The achievements of Hobbs and Sutcliffe are of course common property; not my own, but the whole world's. For ten years or more they partnered each other in representative games of varied importance; their mutual understanding was even more uncanny than their aggregated skills. Their instinct in run-snatching has become legendary; and it was no scurried affair; down went the ball dead at the feet of one from a dead bat and off they went as if someone had pressed a switch. More often than not they were able to stroll the run, so deftly timed were these sporadic excursions from sobriety. Because their partnership had behind it the authority of a representation wider than a local county one, there was a greater weight of public support for them and they attracted a higher intensity of emotional backing than Hobbs and Sandham as Surrey openers ever did. And there were times when they seemed virtually infallible. Gilligan's tour of Australia was not a huge success; but out of the wreckage emerged the triumphant Tate on the one hand and this astonishing opening pair on the other.

Hobbs failed in the last Test, but apart from that they were the brightest composite jewel that the British crown could boast since before the First World War.

Yet their finest hour was to come. You would have thought that the great day in the second Test in 1924-5 would have been difficult to parallel, when facing a total of exactly 600 runs these two batsmen held the crease from dawn till dusk and put 283 on the board before sundown. But that was fair-weather cricket, and by this time Hobbs was tired of that and Sutcliffe was never temperamentally at ease with it. They both liked something to bite on; and the story of the two greatest stands of their lives is the story of two supreme craftsmen working in material for which their craft was not designed—an Oval sticky and, worse, far worse, a Melbourne special.

The story of the Oval Test that brought home the Ashes in 1926 is as familiar as ABC to the addict; it is of particular interest in this context to remember that Australia scraped a lead of 20 or so by the evening of the second day, that Hobbs and Sutcliffe made it good with a little to spare that same night and that it rained like a reminiscence of the Flood all night long and, clearing up under sun in the morning, converted the shirt-front Oval wicket into a conglomeration of hogspudding and gravel-rash. On the bowling side were Gregory, Mailey, Grimmett, Arthur Richardson, Macartney. On the batting side were a formidable list of names with a rather less than formidable record against this bowling. Hendren and Woolley are wonderful names to say over; but at this time they formed in the England batting order what might possibly be termed, justly enough, an undistributed middle; backing them were all-rounders of real merit, Tate, Rhodes, Geary, Stevens, whose batting was less fearsome than their bowling, and a glad captain, Chapman, who might get a hundred or might get a duck. It was up to Hobbs and Sutcliffe to keep this gallimaufry from the wicket until the pitch was at least humanly predictable; and in the teeth of these frightening bowlers they did just that. They are reputed to have used all manner of wiles and skills that were never in the book or out of it, to have kidded the bowlers whom they wanted to face that they were in their last extreme of despair to encourage them to stay on and prevent the real menaces from bowling; still, whatever usages they adopted they wore down the barbs in the attack until the wicket dried out; and they stayed until after lunch and pulled England to safety and finally to victory.

That was something indeed; but it was nothing to the horrific task they were set at Melbourne two years later; when on a real stinker of a wicket, beside which the Oval on that classic morning was like a practice pitch at a great public school, England were required to go in after lunch to make over 300, with all their wickets standing. Reputable unbiased judges, sober and Christian men, declared on their oath that England would not get 60; and this team was an improvement on that at the Oval; it had Hammond at the very peak of his greatness and Jardine at his canniest to follow; there was no deprecation of their skill. It was just considered impossible by anybody and everybody, that is all. England would not get 60.

In the teeth of this situation Hobbs and Sutcliffe proved beyond doubt that there have never been any better players of good bowling on bad wickets in the whole history of the game. They perfected, as only they have ever done, the art of dead-bat play and of leaving ill alone. They were smitten hip and thigh; they were purple with honourable bruises; but they stopped the straight shooters and they kept their bats out of the way, often by the most exquisite and delicate lateness of perception in the world, of the most vicious spinners and kickers with which they were visited. Again they played through all the dirt alone; again they came out triumphant; again they set England firmly on the road to victory. On the wicket where England would not get 60 these two alone reached 105. Supreme skill, supreme judgment, supreme joy in a difficult situation; Hobbs' genius and Sutcliffe's tenacity and spirit.

Sutcliffe possibly possessed this additional ruggedness, allied to great flexibility of wrist and body, to a higher degree than most cricketers. Undoubtedly it gave him an advantage over Sandham, who had character and tenacity in plenty but did not, to the same degree as the Yorkshireman, make a kind of major offensive weapon out of these qualities. Sutcliffe practised, in fact, a powerful deceit; he looked so supremely refined and elegant that his opponents could hardly prepare themselves adequately for the granite imperturbability, the classic immovable obstinacy, that characterized every gesture and movement of his body. He looked like a rather more than usually responsible administrative civil servant; he batted with the angular and canny resolution of a Yorkshire business man. His quiet and handsome presence did not communicate itself completely to his batting, which was quiet indeed but not perhaps handsome, strong rather than graceful. Hobbs was all willow, Sutcliffe all oak. He met the fastest and the most cunning with identical phlegm, playing forward with complete safety with a bat inclined out of the straight, meeting the ball squarely in the middle and completing the stroke with a curious twist of the wrists which had the effect of nailing the ball to the ground and screwing it in. His attacking strokes had the power of perfect timing but many of them looked, even if they were not in effect, faulty. His celebrated hook, which was like a pile-driver's mallet in execution, was an ungraceful affair because of his habit of holding his right arm bent when he swept across the ball's flight; it finished less like a hook than a hoick, but it brought him hundreds of runs. He first began to plague the Australians in 1924, after preliminary forays with South Africa; and although he had ceased to play Test cricket by then, he was still undefeated when rain robbed Yorkshire of a terrific victory over Bradman's side in 1938, proceeding as coolly and menacingly as he had always done, as unmoved by the tension as if he had been batting in his back garden. In 1945 I saw him again in a charity match; he looked exactly as he had looked to me at Hove in 1921, fielding contemplatively on the boundary as George Hirst bowled to Joe Vine. The years never touched Sutcliffe; they merely strengthened him; the only one of Hobbs' many worthy partners on whom sometimes you felt that Hobbs liked to lean.

Hobbs and Sutcliffe—I last saw them open an innings together at Lord's in 1932 in the Gents v. Players match; it must have been one of their very last partnerships. They headed a side that for power and variety beat any Players' side that I can remember to fritters, for after Numbers 1 and 2 came Woolley and Hammond, Hendren and Paynter, Larwood and Tate, Duckworth and Voce and Freeman. What a roll-call, this; what a curious fate for this side to be bowled out not long after tea by Allen, Allom and Peebles, with only Hammond and Paynter giving evidence of their quality in full. Sutcliffe was unusually craggy, and Woolley was

sleepy, as he could often be ; Hobbs made a few deft strokes and
was bowled by a beauty for 24. It was not a resounding farewell.
But Hobbs, very appropriately, seeing that it was I who was being
obliged, performed his old trick that had so exasperated me in the
past. After the Gentlemen, Duleep, Pataudi and Jardine in particular, had spent the next day flogging all over Lord's that Olympian
attack, Hobbs rescued his side by playing all through the third day
an innings of 161 not out that is enshrined in the most sacred annals
of this series. Of course I was not there; I wouldn't be; and I never
again saw him take a bat in his hands.

He did not retire for another year or two. In 1933 (he was fifty)
after a rest he came back to the Oval and hit over 200 against the
brutally fast West Indies slingers and made himself stiff for a week.
Then a year later, he played in George Duckworth's benefit game
at Old Trafford and made his last hundred. Soon after this he faded
out quietly and without fuss; his last innings for Surrey, I regret to
say, was 0. This is the way the world ends.

When I was very much younger, in the fullest flush of my
idolatry for this man, I had often wondered seriously how I could
go on taking an interest in things when he had retired. Well, the
moment came and went; I bore up, having other matters to sustain
my active attention. But now, I wonder, so many years later—how
about himself? Here was, in a restricted context I admit, an artist
of extraordinary skill. He must in the nature of things have derived
incommunicable pleasure from his beautiful exercise of that art.
It must have filled his life. And now, age is upon him, he is Sir
Jack, honoured so happily so many years after his performance—
sure evidence that he has never been forgotten—and his seventieth
birthday brings tributes from all over the world. Vigorous he is,
no doubt, happy in his great achievement and the affection of an
enormous public, but prevented by age from ever again practising
the one thing that made him supreme in his generation—the art
of the cricketer. What must he feel when he handles a bat? Can he
bear it, the memory and the regret together? I do not think I envy
him; there are some ways in which life can be more merciless than
death.

There is, and was, the hero of my youth, kindling me with the
perfection of his performance, setting breathless dizzying standards

for the rest of my life to fall short of. He and his partners made a pattern of cricket excellence in my mind, a pattern of courage and conflict as well as of æsthetic satisfaction; a pattern that, absorbed into my unconscious responses to the game, made my appreciation of it a deeper and more complex experience than a boy or a youth commonly extracts from the worship of his harmless heroes. The barren tale of their achievement is nothing; the assessment of their meaning in my expanding life, with the addition of the new hero-worship I shall now describe, is for me an important stage in my story.

CHAPTER SEVEN

IMPERIAL HAMMOND

ONE day early in the Australian summer of 1928-9 a Press photo-
grapher at Sydney, squinting through his sights for a suitable action
snap, released the shutter at one precise and infinitesimal instant
that gave him (all unknowing, it is to be supposed) the most striking
action picture of a batsman that has ever been put on record.* For
poise, grace, symmetry, composition and power it might be a
picture of a statue by Pheidias; there is a flawless balance in the
distribution of every line and every mass in the field of vision, and
moreover it conveys an infinite potentiality of strength. It is
Hammond at the finish of an off-drive; or, rather, not at the
relaxed finish, like the classic Trumper snap where you can feel the
delicious release of the sprung muscles after contained effort, but
a split instant of time after the maximum of productive tension.
The head, beautifully poised, is still tucked down over the point of
impact; the bat has come up in a great arc to finish over the left
shoulder; the left toe, giving direction to the stroke, is pointed as
lightly and as weightlessly as a ballet dancer's. This dancer's light-
ness, expressed in the poise of the left foot, gives the whole bodily
attitude a strange and lovely ease of movement. I never saw
Nijinsky, but I doubt if any gesture of his could convey the power
and the glory of motion as this superb snapshot of Walter Hammond
does. Compositionally the picture has built itself up most happily
in the form of a pyramid; the wicket-keeper, who is Oldfield and
therefore adds an instinctive grace of his own, is bent alertly in such
a way that the line of his back and the transverse one of his arms and
outstretched gloves exactly lead into and answer the corresponding
lines of the batsman's figure. All these lines point to the centre;

* It appears as a frontispiece to this book; but unhappily the only surviving print
omits the wicket-keeper.

to the great shoulders and whipcord sinews at the hub of this explosive activity. All else is just as the imagination hears and sees, the rich thunderous crack and the red flash, and the straight line shot through the covers to the fence.

More often than not, when pictures of Hammond are required, that is the one that does duty; and it is appropriate enough, for it shows him on the very threshold of his greatest period of renown. All in all his career in first-class cricket lasted from 1920, when he played, I think, three matches, to 1951, when he emerged from a sickeningly early retirement to play one more; yet it never excelled in consistency of success the greatness of his tour of Australia in 1928-9 under Percy Chapman. In the series of five Tests he made 905 runs, a record were it not for Bradman, who hardly counts; he seemed unbeatable and unbowlable and, though he curbed them of necessity, he commanded ferocious aggressive powers, of which the epitome is for all to see in the magnificent photograph I have described. On that tour he entered into possession of a kingdom for which, seasons before, he had begun to make insistent bids. I say " kingdom " with considered stress on the word; about him and his cricket was a perennial air of cool domination. Where Hobbs seemed *primus inter pares*, chief servant of the state in an idyllic republic, Hammond lorded it unabashed like an emperor. I know nothing of his personal temperament; from hints I have gathered here and there he seems to have been gifted with a modesty and charm which make his public character even more attractive; but as a public figure he displayed the pride of a commander, a pride without frills and flounces, a direct and uncontradictable pride. " Hammond," said Denzil Batchelor, " never walked to the wicket. He strode "; and when he came down the steps and out on to the grass, you could hear in your ears the trumpets and the drums of an imperial salutation. His very name sounded like a ceremonial discharge of cannon.

He was not tall, but in his youth he was so proportioned as to give the effect of height together with a sinuous mobility concealing strength. I saw him first in a Champion County match at the Oval in 1925, in a team resplendent with all the batting talents, where his place was at seven or eight. For Gloucestershire he had had a false start, owing to qualification trouble, and on resuming after an interval had begun to impress everyone with the astonishing power and correctness of his back play, his intensely aggressive off-side hitting, and (thrown in as if casually) bowling and fielding beyond the useful. That same season he had roused Northern hackles by battering into impotent pulp, on its own ground, a Lancashire attack which included Macdonald, Dick Tyldesley and Parkin, to the value of 250 runs. In the match I saw his batting performance was negligible, and in any case I did not see it; but he bowled with an exciting swirling run-up and arched action; and he stood close up in the slips and held on to a buzzing cut with a practised ease that I was to get to know.

That winter he went on a tour to the West Indies, collected over 200 in an unofficial Test match, and came home with a serious illness that put him on his back during the crucial year of 1926 when he would otherwise have been fledging himself against the Australians. I, who under the spell of Hobbs took little note of him, let him slip from my memory and concentrated on the main issues; one young batsman the more or less did not matter. Hobbs, Sutcliffe and Rhodes had won us the Ashes, and what need had I to grieve for the loss of a promising all-rounder? It was true that when the next season began I looked for his return with some interest, remembering his great promise and feeling for him in an ordeal, that of re-establishing his confidence in himself, that must have been at that crucial stage in his career (he was not yet 24) a rather unnerving one.

He answered my interested curiosity in the best possible manner. It was a filthy season, strewn with rains and ruins, a tattered squally ragbag of a summer conspicuous for abandonments and butt-ends of drowned cricket matches; it abides in my memory (I was in the 4th XI at school, batting nervously and ineffectively, and I remember it well) as canopied with low racing clouds and bespattered with vile blowing showers. In this shambles of a season Walter Hammond came back into the game and instantly scored a thousand runs in May. His long rest had filled out his figure and, apparently, given him renewed confidence. From the very first match, which was against Yorkshire, he laid into the bowling with a power quite out of this world; it was in this dim and dripping May of 1927 that cricket first found itself enriched by the storming beauty of those murderous off-drives. Many can now remember the iron summer of 1947 and the bushels of runs gathered in by Edrich and Compton on the brown baked grounds on the sweating sweltering afternoons of high June. We held our breath at their rapacity then, it is true, but it was nothing to the sensation that hit us like a planet twenty years before under the curtains of cloud, as Hammond in his billowing shirt with buttoned-down sleeves raced to his thousand between the freezing showers. Yorkshire, Lancashire, Surrey, Middlesex—all were met and massacred; and if the unconscionable weather had not entirely collapsed in June he would have tacked on another thousand by the end of that month to match the fruits of the first. In that marvellous first season of his true fulfilment he was established for good and all as one of the great. From that time forward he never lost his place in the world's esteem or in mine; and from the first Test in the next season against the West Indies at Lord's, until the last Test in 1946 against India at the Oval when I saw him bat for the last time on a cheerless windy wet day in just such another season as that of his first blaze of splendour, no England side, in England, ever took the field without him, save once when he was suffering from throat trouble and could not be considered.

Of the thousands of runs he made, wickets he took, catches he snatched; of his fantastic all-round capabilities, reaching their Everest in that impossible Cheltenham week in 1928, when in the match beginning on the Wednesday, against Surrey, he made 139 and 143, got Hobbs caught, and himself took ten catches in his opponents' two innings; and in the match following, on the Saturday, made a casual 80 and then took nine Worcester wickets for 23 and caught the odd man, rounding off the performance with 6 for 105 in the second innings—of these and of all the cumulative glories that resembled and transcended them, I do not mean to speak in detail. They belong to the historian and to the statistician, and Hammond fed them both with a most royal bounty. But these performances, like those of Hobbs and all my other heroes, are written down elsewhere more succinctly than I could write them. G. K. Chesterton, who never wrote about Hammond, remarked in an essay on Robert Louis Stevenson that a man's life is held to mean what he did, the whole external pantomime of his existence; but this (he goes on) is in fact the most lifeless part of him, being the farthest remove from the centre of life. I believe that to be true, in large measure, of great cricketers. The external pantomime of their scores and their aggregate is a pointer to their quality, but it conveys no indication of the essence of that quality itself. I could go on for pages piling up descriptions of Hammond's centuries and Hammond's toll of wickets, but unless I can inform that tale with a spice or a suggestion of the quality that differentiated this great master from others as great or greater then it would be little better than a series of chalk-marks scored on a barn door; one chalk-mark as good as the next. Two different runs look much like one another in the score-book or in *Wisden*; two different centuries, too; even two different batches of a hundred centuries; they astound in bulk, and the senses soon tire of mere bulk.

Chesterton's remark about a man's life and its relevance to his being is true for my purpose; his later remark in the same essay that "we should not learn [Stevenson's] real greatness from his quality; we can only learn his real greatness from his quantity," is for my purposes as patently misleading. Hammond enjoyed quantity as few batsmen in cricket have ever enjoyed it; but since fortune blessed me with attendance at an infinitesimally small proportion of the quantity, it cannot have been that quantity that gave me my lifelong admiration of his greatness. I think I can claim that he would have impressed me as deeply as in fact he did if I had seen him do nothing but play a maiden over. He impressed me, in a sense, more than any other cricketer impressed me; the idea, the plain idea of Walter Hammond still shivers my spine, as some are shivered by a trumpet call. Yet consistently, during that career of flaming success, I was disappointed of results. I have told how I chased Hobbs for years unavailingly; I chased Hammond all his life. Yet he did not bilk me of his quality; I had all the evidence I needed of that, and am convinced and content. All else that I was greedy for, and unsatisfied of, was the luxury of superfluity. He gave that to others in plenty and running over; he never gave it to me. What he did give me was an abiding vision of an art and a personality some-how fused; compact, commanding, confident; the superb mastering of physical and mental forces to the execution of a balanced and beautiful action, and series of actions. He radiated authority.

There never was an athlete, in his younger days especially, so lightly and delicately poised; yet there was no tension in his attitude, only a limber felicitous disposal of the limbs in poses that seemed to fall instinctively into attitudes of grace. His delicacy had nothing of affectation about it; it was a muscular strength that carried with it not a pose or a presumption. He stood in the slips on legs planted firmly, rather wide apart, the body flexing from the hips, the hands alert; his walk from one end of the wicket to the other was enough to reveal the grace of those compact muscles; his cap slightly askew, his nose in the air, he distilled a certain detached indifference into his manner. When he came to bat he injected into this detachment a suspicion of what might be called hostility; the better the opposition the intenser this became. On rare and special occasions it was reinforced by a flavour of insolent contempt. His eyes narrowed; as he stood at the wicket he seemed all shoulder and bat and pad. And when he moved from the static to the dynamic his feet slid as quietly and as inevitably as a dancer's dancing in tune. As the years proceeded and his frame thickened there seemed no corresponding slowing down of his footwork; only an increasingly obvious source of power behind the stroke, where previously there had been surprise at the stinging unexpectedness of its violence.

Two particular strokes of his I do remember out of the long panorama of the innings I saw him play; neither of them strokes for which he was renowned. Eleven years separated them; September 1928, on the eve of his great progress through Australia, and August 1939, on the eve of something quite other. On the first occasion, willowy and fresh with the assurance of powerful youth, coming in after Hobbs and Woolley in a thunderous batting order for the Rest of England against Lancashire the champion county, he received in his first over a rasping breakback from Macdonald off the line of the middle and off stumps. It was a swine of a ball to have to counter so early in his innings; it would have picked the leg stump from behind most batsmen before they were aware of its lethal last-minute dip. Hammond tucked his nose down over it and glanced it clean off the bat's middle for four, a stroke that he did not play often and which with the apotheosis of the inswinger and the leg trap few batsmen remember to use nowadays. The ball glittered like a jewel as it went to the rails in a streak; and although he was caught at the wicket not many minutes later, and a fabulous innings built itself around our ears with centuries by Hobbs and Sutcliffe and Hendren, and various lashings-about by Woolley and Leyland and Ames, yet that one stroke is the sole enduring legacy, for me, of the day's play.

I sat in the pavilion then, high behind his back; eleven years later family necessities had stronger demands and I had discontinued my membership; and I watched the last first-class match that the Oval staged before Hitler invaded Poland from the bob seats alongside the Vauxhall stand, far in the distance and remote from my accustomed contacts. In this last Test match the West Indies strove and stormed with some success to break an England side that harboured the remnants of the one that had beaten Australia on that ground twelve months before; and Hammond for a long time made strangely heavy weather of fast bowlers, notably Constantine and Martindale, whose bite was every bit as bad as their bark. All of a sudden, out of a patch of somnolence, came a thunderbolt of memorable force. Hammond had leaned back and hit a short ball on the off stump with fearful power into the unguarded areas about long-on—down to my very feet, in fact. I have rarely seen a ball travel quicker; at one moment it was going normally down the pitch from the bowler to the batsman; at the next it was fearsomely among us, cutting a smoking path through the grass. Just an ordinary pull, but with the impact of a steam-hammer.

It may be that these isolated strokes surprised and dazzled by their unexpectedness, and that it is on that account that they have outlived in my memory the more characteristic delights with which he normally adorned his play. It was true of Hobbs that his strokes all round the wicket were so consummately skilful that he did not possess one that materially outshone the others, nor were any of the normal orthodoxies lacking; and that therefore you thought of Hobbs without particular reference to any one favourite shot, but in the context mostly of his departure from the usual, as I have done already in this book. It would not have been wrong to say the same of Hammond: I have a photograph of a match in Australia in 1928 in which he has just executed the most delicate tickle of a late cut; he excelled in the towering full-shouldered clump straight back over the bowler's head, with which he once hit the ball clean through the pavilion door at Lord's and landed it first bounce crack against the far wall of the Long Room; and, as I have already shown, a leg-glide of his is immortal in my memory. The difference between him and a master like Hobbs was that no wile of bowler, eccentricity of pitch or vicissitude of game could ever induce the latter to drop a single stroke out of his repertoire; he used them all with great safety and penetration, whatever the circumstances. Hammond, on the other hand, felt compelled to trim his sails to the prevailing wind; and it is said that experience of one kind and another led him quite early in his career to dispense with the hook. At least that is what we are told, and I admit I did not, so far as I can remember, see him execute this stroke; yet there remains the wry remark of Robertson-Glasgow to the effect that Hammond may possibly have dispensed with the hook but he had never noticed the lack of it when he bowled him a long hop. But if he did go lightly on certain on-side shots it is a matter of resonant history that he made up for it on the off.

Between backward point and mid-off Hammond is for all time undisputed king. On the ground or in the air they went from the rich middle of his bat like bombs. His methods of attack varied, his footwork never. That was always light and pliant, manœuvring his powerful frame to a nicety at a split second's notice; but in attack he would bring into play the colossal tension of his great shoulders and reinforce it with the whipped uncoiling of his wrists—or he would stand erect and use the wrists alone, as he levered the shot off his back foot with all the muscular power that he could gather into the action. If he went out and drove off the front foot, God help mid-off or extra cover if it went along the ground and they got a touch to it; it must have been like being handed for a moment or so a ladleful of melted steel. More often it would beat all fielders running all ways, or if he raised his head a fraction early, as he sometimes did, it would whizz like a golfer's drive over extra cover's head with a strong bending swing to it; at other times it went straight, with a long hanging carry. But the gem was the upstanding slash off the back foot. Bowl Hammond a quick good-length ball on the off stump or outside it and either mid-off, extra cover or cover himself would have to dash or dive; bowl the same ball farther up or shorter, it did not matter, and he would crack it square as it passed him, rising on his toes and thrashing across the flight with an uncanny precision of timing, so that fielders with their heels on the very fence were lucky if they had moved when the ball hit the rails. Woolley's off-drives were perhaps smoother and sweeter; but for power and glory and grace Hammond's off-side play was the major delight of twentieth-century cricket.

I am one of his most devoted, not to say fanatical, admirers; and yet the full irony of frustration was reserved for me by fate; before me indeed his superb panoply of batsmanship was never displayed in its full splendour. I saw his greatness fitfully like the sun on a cloudy day. As for so many tantalizing years Jack Hobbs had done, so Hammond excelled in incredible feats the day before or the day after I watched him vainly for full measure of success. The first time I saw him in the full tide of his mature greatness, in his destroying summer of 1927, he had (would you believe it?) been out the very last thing the night before, the very last thing. Later in the barren day he came out to field with the rest, impeccably laundered I remember, and treading with the assurance that he was beginning to wear as a trade mark; but I never saw him bat that season, and in the next, when he was if anything even more consistent, I watched him scrape 3 two days before he launched himself on that fantastic week of all-round proficiency at Cheltenham of which I have already made breathless mention. Then in his last innings before he went through Australia like a withering flame I saw him make 9. On the one occasion in the next season when I saw him bat he was caught one-handed in the slips for 8.

For better or worse this kind of experience continued throughout his career. I did see him make one century, and a satisfying proportion of another; and I would like a pound note for every day on which I had leisure to watch him in the field. In the early part of his career indeed their was plenty of opportunity to consider him as a bowler; and I accept these visions of his out-cricket as valuable substitutes in my own experience for the prime satisfaction of watching him at his batting. For Hammond's greatness was spread evenly over all his play; it was in his slip fielding as much as in his batting, in his bowling as much as in either of the other two. By this I do not intend to write him down as a great bowler—only as a great cricketer bowling, who could indicate by his bowling that

he was out of the ordinary, even if his bowling was not. And sometimes it was. His bowling had the Hammond mark of assured
distinction upon it. His action was the most beautiful I have ever
seen among medium-paced bowlers; for grace and felicity Larwood
and Macdonald were better among fast men and Verity among the
slows, but Hammond's run-up like a bird's flight curve, and the
splendid arching back of his body as he went into his action, were
only extensions, variations, comments indeed on his great cover-
drive or his back-foot slash. He swung the new ball viciously away
from the bat and he was said to come off the pitch as unexpectedly
quickly as Maurice Tate. An all-rounder of such commanding vigour and competence as Hammond could not fairly be expected to
practise all departments of the game with equal assiduity, and it was
his bowling that quite fairly and naturally was allowed to fall into
disuse. It was a young man's art; and if I want to recapture quickly
to my imagination the young Hammond it is that swallow-swerve
run-up I remember most readily and the arched enchantment of the
free light action following it.

The rest of his art he preserved unjaded into near middle age. It
is a deplorable chance, and I believe it to be only a chance, that
decreed that on the tour of Australia which concluded his career
he should have been in his own special context a failure. We think
of him therefore as petering out and retiring not a moment too
soon. We forget that in the streaming wet season of 1946, the prelude to his last tour, he topped the English averages by the height of
the stratosphere with an average of over 80. We forget that he had
just as disastrous a Test series as far back as 1934; we forget easily
enough that his performance on the ill-fated tour gave him an all-
over average of 41 and included two masterpieces of innings of
32 and 23 on the spitting swamp of a Brisbane wicket where hardly
anybody else got double figures. It is true that in the Tests that
followed he did not do very well; but there were preoccupations
in his mind, and he was leading a side of patchy and experimental
quality. Let us remind ourselves that in what was virtually his last
first-class match, a Test against New Zealand (though twice later
he played in first-class games, one of which was as recent as 1951),
he scored a splendid and selfless 79 and held a peach of a catch at
slip.

A peach of a catch at slip; almost an inevitability when Hammond was playing. In the early part of his career he paraded the covers and the outfield, and I have seen him sprint like a stag with a real runner's rhythmic action to cut off a four; but all his Test match days were spent at slip, and as for Gloucester—what Charlie Parker owed to him is only matched by what he owed to Charlie Parker. Close up on the bat's shoulder for Parker; back fifteen yards for Larwood, within chatting distance of the wicket-keeper; for twenty years that was his inevitable post. In Test match action pictures from 1928 to 1947, with England in the field, there he is, receptive and alert, cheek by jowl with Ames or Duckworth or Evans, flanked by Chapman or Hendren or Compton. In action pictures of Bradman or Woodfull or McCabe or Barnes, there he is brooding in the background, distinctive, unfussy, virtually infallible. It was highly characteristic of him that he never in his life made a spectacular catch, though it is probable he took a hundred or two in his time that no one else could have touched. Where Chapman, wonderful fielder, might have hurled his vast weight sideways and flicked the ball one-handed an inch from the grass while rolling desperately over, Hammond would have taken the very same catch in his two hands, ankle height, to suit himself, with apparently time to roll up his sleeves first. Those exquisite light feet had taken him by anticipation plumb into the right place as the bat met the ball. He was the greatest slip fielder I have ever watched, and I watched him for long enough. He could absorb a cannon-ball slash or pick a bounding snick off the bat's corner with an air of deepest unconcern.

Although not without gifts of showmanship, he was without showiness. He excelled, in the field, at understatement. In this manner he understated his way to over 800 catches in his career; of which one, a most uncommon affair, I remember to this instant as a blazing masterpiece. It was in a Test against India in 1936; in which, after ascertaining that I would not be present until the next day, he made 217. In the second innings of India in which many brave and inexperienced attempts were made, notably I remember by Amar Singh, to hit the not very formidable England attack off its length, a rather erratic G. O. Allen was bowling with great energy to a very erratic and equally energetic Mushtaq Ali—a batsman of freedom and beauty whose charm was expansive and

evanescent, like candy-floss. This good batsman, faced with a rearing long hop outside the off-stump, thrashed heartily across the line
without bothering to get his foot to it, with the result that instead
of going through cover like one of Hammond's own specials it
rocketed at fearful speed at the height of about eight feet through the
gap between first and second slip, standing I thought a little on the
close side for a bowler of Allen's pace. Second slip was Voce, and
the ball was by him in a blink, going like the dogs of war; but
instinctively he leapt to it, grunting, at full stretch of his left arm,
and as luck ordained got a touch on it with, I take it, his stretched
little finger. The deflection was instantaneous and dramatic; the
ball ricocheted like a shot off a shovel in the rough direction of the
square-leg umpire; from eight feet in the air it shot steeply down-
wards like the hypotenuse of a rather erect right-angled triangle,
its speed hardly decreased and its power to disconcert unexpectedly
augmented. Hammond at first slip pivoted gracefully on his right
foot, and with his back to the wicket and the batsman gathered in the
catch just below his right armpit, one-handed, as it sped across his
chest on the way to the opposite boundary. The surprise was not
for the breathless speed of the manœuvre, which was indeed breathless enough, but for the fact that Hammond accepted it as if it were
part of some pre-rehearsed ritual carried out with care and elegance
and watchfulness, but with no possible need for haste or surprise.

   What was it about this man without warmth, this detached artist
with the heavy-lidded eyes, this ruthless and efficient destroyer,
to endear him so closely to his public? Jack Hobbs had the common
touch and the common humours; Hammond, in public at least,
walked like an emperor and walked alone. Yet England and English
crowds thrilled to him as to few others; the welcoming roars
broke more violently round his indifferent head than they did
round any of his contemporaries. They tried to effect familiar
relationships by calling him Wally. This may have been all right
for his private character, but as far as his public face is concerned
it was, for me, like calling Dr. Johnson Sammy. For me he is always
Walter Hammond; stern and majestic names for a stern and majestic
man. Yet on his very last appearance, in 1951, when he played for
Gloucestershire against Somerset in the August Bank Holiday game,
he confessed that he had been hardly able to see the first few balls

bowled to him, so moved had he been by the tremendous reception given him by the crowd. Abiding admiration, yes; immense respect, yes. But popularity, affection, a welcome to stir the heart? It is strange, and it is very good. It shows beyond doubt that the British public recognized and warmed to the character and artistry of an unusual man, not caring whether he troubled to pay court to them with his personality or not.

For Walter Hammond brought to the highest reaches of the game a stability and an assurance administered with stunning power. Nothing that he did was without grace; nothing that he did was without authority. He was orthodox, but he expressed his orthodoxy in rich chorded tones. His on-drive was right out of the book; his off-drive was right out of this world. To magnify the good and the right to Titanic dimensions; this is to behave after the high Roman fashion. Jack Hobbs was a fifth-century Greek; Walter Hammond an imperial Roman, of the days of the great Augustan empire. The Latin language has come down to us with its four great qualities plain: clarity, strength, weight, precision. Those, in his lesser field, are Walter Hammond's qualities too.

Let us put it another way. English poetry and English batsmanship, comparable whether they be or not, are both bred of the English character and they both in their diverse development took historical courses that can be regarded as parallel. Chaucer and W. G. Grace were alike in hewing a fine and delicate art out of the bits and pieces of a pastime, giving it strength, humour, flexibility, endurance and beauty; and each was followed in good time by a transcendent genius to seize on the potentialities of what the other had left behind and play superhuman and immortal tricks with them. Chaucer was succeeded by Shakespeare, W. G. Grace by Jack Hobbs. Next in the sequence, and finally for the purpose of this analogy, comes an artist of a different kind, weighty, authoritative and profound, to take the bright colours of genius and tame them to an orthodoxy of infinite possibility; making out of their random and unending hints a tradition that, stabilized, will effect the art's development for centuries. Chaucer and Shakespeare had John Milton; W. G. and Hobbs had Walter Hammond. (Now, perhaps it is possible to understand why I find it difficult to think of him as Wally, once the Miltonic setting of his batsmanship has been established.) Proust has said that "les vrais paradis sont les paradis qu'on a perdus." Maybe; but the thought, even for a few reminiscent moments only, of the character and authority of this immortal cricketer is a batsman's paradise, regained.

It is not given often to an idolater to meet his idols face to face, and it is as well that it is so, because he will either be disappointed in the experience or behave so idiotically that he will know in his heart for ever after that his idol thought him a fool. It would be misleading if I were to conclude this account of the two great masters of my worship without recording that some years after I had reached what is normally regarded as an age of discretion I went into Jack Hobbs' shop to buy a bat and was shown into the store-room into the very breathing presence of the man himself, who with the greatest good will and courtesy in the world proceeded to devote the next half-hour of his life to selling me one. I teetered before him in a helpless daze, uttering what I trust were recognizable noises at appropriate stages in the dialogue, and when we finally fixed on a bat and he said, "Yes, sir, I think you'll get a lot of pleasure out of that one," I would cheerfully have died in an ecstasy there and then. (The fact that the article split after I had used it three or four times is referable to unskilled use rather than to over-slick salesmanship.) He then glanced at the tie I was wearing, which showed him that I had been to school where his brother and his friend had been successive groundsmen, and gave me unsolicited discount on the spot. I had breath enough to stammer out my appreciation, and staggered out into Fleet Street in a haze of beatitude.

With Walter Hammond I have no such contact. I have met people who have played with him, and once crossed the path, very indirectly, of a girl who was said to have met him at a party. But the closest link I have with him is far more believable and far more ridiculous. My friend Leslie Johnson, the keenest non-playing cricketer in Nature, as excited as a third-former over the minutest details of the game at an age when he should be thinking of his latter end, came to me in a quiver of uncontrollable excitement one day and told me that he had just discovered that he was living next door to Hammond's aunt. I said that I didn't believe him and that he was to go away and think up something better; but he persisted in this ridiculous yarn, which sounded like something out of a book by Robertson-Glasgow, and at length I was convinced that it was true. And so it is. I suppose Hammond is entitled to an aunt, and if this is so, I suppose that it is in the natural order of things that she should live next door to somebody, and there seems no reason why that somebody should not be a friend of mine. She is apparently a very nice old lady, and Hammond's cousin, her other nephew, comes in and mows the lawn for her from time to time. Admirable; but how *queer*, how very *queer* to be able to say " You know Hammond? Yes, *the* Hammond, the very great Hammond. Well, I know a man who lives next door to his aunt."

CHAPTER EIGHT

A LA RECHERCHE DU TEMPS PERDU

HOBBS has gone; Hammond has gone; in the destroying fullness
of the years Compton, Hutton, Bedser will go too. It is not a very
happy or reconciling thought. The days of a man's age are three-
score years and ten, and, with the help of antibiotics and the most
up-to-date lotions and potions, a little more; and for some of us all
but the first eight or nine of those years are fired with a consuming
love for the trappings of this game. Let us assume then that for
over sixty years, if we are fortunate enough to retain our faculties
for all that time, we shall watch and judge at first or second hand
the public progress of its greatest protagonists; that means that
we shall outlive four whole generations, that we shall again and
again have to temper our enthusiastic enjoyments with repeated
mourning for the lost Hornbys and Barlows of our golden youth.
I hope and pray that the eyes with which I look out upon Lord's
for the last time will retain undimmed, subject to the necessary
ravages of the years, the quickened and absorbed delight with which
they saw it first, on the opening morning of the Test match against
South Africa in 1924. "Have you seen A. P. F. Chapman at the
nets?" squealed with immense excitement a schoolboy friend of
mine with whom I came bewilderingly face to face some quarter
of an hour before play began. "No," I said enviously. "He was
marvellous [or ripping, or topping, or super, or whatever stood in
for an appreciative superlative in those springtime days]—he was
marvellous. Getting right out to the ball every time." And he
vanished in the crowd making for its seats, in the days before the
tiled Grand Stand arose to face the towering chimney, and before
Father Time first bent dourly to remove his ironic bail. And in due
time out came England to field, and the fresh young Chapman,
adventurous and handsome, fielded with them all day, the athlete's

and the schoolboy's dream. And the day's play ended, and the match, and the season, and other seasons, and the old Grand Stand came down and the new one went up, with Father Time upon it, and the sun sloped behind the Tavern and the plane trees shivered and rustled over the practice ground certain years; and Chapman and his youthful glory rose and prospered and declined with all the rest of that field full of folk; until there came seasons when he most decidedly failed to get right out to the ball every time, flashed and flicked at it in fact like the low-handicap golfer he was, and beat the air and got caught in the slips and suffered disappointment and failure like all of us who watched him on that first morning; and at last Lord's saw him no more, and he became a memory, a pleasant and lively one indeed, but still a memory, together with the England captain he succeeded and the England captain who succeeded him. Yet Lord's is still there, and I go on the first morning of a Test match with the identical quiver at my stomach that had me in its grip that June morning thirty years ago; and I look out with the same eyes on the rolled and waiting pitch, and I hear and contribute to the buzz and chatter as schoolboy meets schoolboy and ejaculates in an excited yelp, " Have you seen Graveney at the nets? It was marvellous [or smashing, or wizard, or supersonic, or sheer-lined or whatever obnoxious epithet passes now for the highest meed of praise]. It was marvellous. Getting right out to the ball every time."

These eyes are the same, and barring certain structural alterations which do not much matter, Lord's is the same. And the game, as I tried to insist in the first chapter of all, is the same as well. Only the players change. Therefore we are presented with the illusion of a constant watcher of a constant background, marking dutifully off as they pass before his eyes the only elements in the scene which vary. If they did not vary, there would be no Time. Their variations are the only means of marking Time off, in the context of the game. Just as in the fine phrase of Anatole France, Zola was a moment in the conscience of man, so Hendren, let us say, was a moment in the progress of cricket. And a wonderful moment too; and in this connection it is with a deadly aptness that I record that when at Hastings in 1947 I caught a glimpse of his grinning face in the crowd, and told a little knot of knowledgeable boys around me who it was that I had just seen, they stared one and all and said with an innocence that nigh broke my heart, " Who's Patsy Hendren? "

His moment, for them, had passed unnoticed; and noticed or not they do not fail to go by. Some have moments unusually, deceptively prolonged. Jack Hobbs was in big cricket before my parents were married; he left it not many months all told before I was married myself. My grandfather at the end of his life could have seen Hammond begin his Gloucester career; my son at the age of twelve could have seen him end it. The length of their time lent temporary stability to their state; the hands of the remorseless clock seemed for the moment, for a few moments, to have halted. Yet we looked away for a minute, and the hands had moved; and we had to face Surrey and England without Hobbs, Gloucester and England without Hammond. It was no accidental quirk, but a symbolic comment harbouring a profound and biting irony, that prompted the architect of the new Grand Stand at Lord's to crown it, without the foreknowledge of the committee who commissioned it, with his own immortal flourish—the dim figure of Father Time. In front of him and below him the figures blink and change, blink and change; to the superficial sight the changeless game, simple and elaborate, white against green, goes on for ever in its unruffled harmony; and we the spectators spanning contentedly our four generations of cricketers, watching George Hirst pass, and Hobbs pass, and Sutcliffe pass, and Hammond pass, absorb the comfortable illusion that they alone, the unwavering eyes, are changeless entirely and will remain; while all the day and night Father Time moves to and fro on his roof. He may not have all the answer; but he has the laugh on us.

> But we dream we are rooted in earth—Dust!
> Flesh falls within sight of us, we, though our flower the same
> Wave with the meadow, forget that there must
> The sour scythe cringe, and the blear share come.

So the moments, one after the other, go; and in desperation I try sometimes to nail them on the wing. It isn't easy; concentrate on it as I may, this kind goeth not forth but by prayer and fasting. The moments, whether they be the whole lives of cricketers or the

interval between one ball and another, are elusive under the micro-
scope; they will not be detached, they preserve their independence,
they return to the questioning mind at their own pleasure not
at his, as to the young Proust tasting the madeleine unwitting.
And all attempts to pin and preserve them are, by consequence,
dangerous.

> *He who bends to himself a joy*
> *Doth the winged life destroy.*

All right; it were best to leave well alone. But if my memory
serves me correctly, Blake went on to another couplet, and I do
not see why I should not take up its hint.

> *But he who kisses the joy as it flies*
> *Lives in Eternity's sunrise.*

That is more promising. The only question remaining is this:
whether, if I seek to entrap for contemplation and refreshment one
of these moments (of whichever sort) out of the living procession
of the game that means so much to me, I am doing the first or the
second. Do I, by recapturing a joy, bend it and distort it to my own
requirements so wantonly as to paralyse the winged life? Or can I
take it in such a fashion as not to abuse it, so that through a little
contemplation of this moment in Time I can be given a glimpse,
as Blake suggests, of the illumination of Eternity? I can only try;
and I can try through the valuable medium of one of these moments
which I have had the undeserved luck to be able to intercept before
it has gone—to see it, as it were, in its progression between the past
and the future; a curious little sequence which can act, for me, as
the symbol conveniently to hand for conjectures far more nebulous
though still connected with the theme that is occupying me.

It is appropriate that the scene is Lord's, and that over the whole
progress of this narrative Father Time should be brooding as the
most conspicuous constant. Lord's on a fresh overcast Whit
Monday a few years before the war, ringed with 15,000 Bank Holiday spectators, green after late rain, spruce white paintwork the
highest light in a comparatively colourless landscape. As always
at Whitsun, Sussex are the traditional opponents; a Sussex still with
the tang of my old sea-salt sensation upon them, a Sussex tanned and

sunny from long association with blue sea and burnt sandy beaches, at this time a strong and varied county of optimism and adventure, with red-faced Harry Parks and his tubby smiling brother, the graceful and diffident James Langridge and the solid angular John; Cornford the bowler and Cornford the wicket-keeper, the cheerful active Cook and the cheerful active Wensley, all captained by the slim and distinguished Alan Melville, years later to lead South Africa; but chief among them the distinctive conspicuous legendary Tate, bowling in his forties as if he were under twenty-one.

On a rain-docked Saturday Sussex had made 185, and on this chilly Bank Holiday morning under light clouds Middlesex began deplorably. Tate from the pavilion end bit from the green pitch like a snake striking; he got a wicket in the first quarter of an hour, and after Cornford had secured another before the morning was forty-five minutes old, Tate seemed to gather his huge physical resources for one of his last but one of his greatest bowling performances. As the score, mainly through the lone efforts of that excellent and unrewarded journeyman Hart, crept with difficulty into the forties, Tate struck decisively again. Hendren snicked an outswinger to Cornford; Hulme next ball was most positively and brutally bowled all over his wicket; and after Robins had theatrically saved a hat trick with a mad dash of a single which as near as makes no odds ran Hart out, Tate upset Hart's wicket with a beautiful break-back before he had had time to recover his breath. Middlesex 48 for 5; 137 behind, and Tate had collected in that last cataclysmic over three wickets for one run.

Middlesex lay before him with its back broken; but there was always a tail, apparently unaffected by spinal injuries. Robins characteristically chose this moment for an attacking innings; he hit Cornford off his length, and did his best with the rather more intractable Tate. At the other end was a solid club cricketer named Benka, admirably brave in adversity, who kept his nose down and a broad bat straight; and he it was who survived, for Robins hit Parks an almighty clump and was gloriously caught by Cook under Father Time with both hands above his head, and Benka and a rather younger Sims than I have since become accustomed to went on with some highly valuable consolation.

Highly valuable, but not valuable enough. Wensley bowled

Benka for 22, and the enormous circus act of Jim Smith came roundly into play. He hit several fours off the inside edge and one or two more off the middle; but he got out as he had always looked likely to do, and there was nothing to come but an injured G. O. Allen and some substitute newcomer or other, and Middlesex were still 25 short of the first innings objective. Allen when he came in at number ten (he had dislocated a finger) batted tentatively but with confidence; but with the score at, I think, somewhere in the late 160s, Tate got Sims to snick a slip catch to Parks, and nine wickets were gone and nothing but a crippled man and a boy to stand in the breach.

Well, in came the boy, spruced up and looking new and nervous, to face Tate of all people, bowling at his ferocious best. Allen had a word with him as he came, and the boy nodded, striding off down the pitch bravely to do this distasteful duty. Tate bowled and he played jerkily back and missed; Tate bowled again and he played jerkily back and missed again. At the other end Allen, clearly yearning for the strike, made nervous deprecatory gestures. The boy shook his head as if the flies were at it; played desperately forward at the next ball and got it clearly in the middle. To all our relief that was the last ball of the over.

Allen and the boy, coolly, confidently, without a semblance of a chance or a slip, hit off those necessary runs. The boy showed confidence, clarity and a neat shot to leg; after the first shivering over he was as poised as Allen himself. They hit off the runs and they hit off some more; and when Parks got the boy l.b.w. for 14 he had made about as many as Allen himself had made during the partnership and was cheered back to the pavilion by a delighted crowd as pleased as Punch, his first innings for the county having provided a salty memory that would last him quite a little time. He was only seventeen and what his ambitions were I do not know; but his name was Compton, Denis Compton, and before the end of the next season he was going in Number 5 for England.

I watched him from time to time at Lord's and the Oval that season and the next, and the one or two more that intervened before the world broke up in broil. I watched him and I took to him, a slim, cheerful fresh-faced lad shiny with satisfied keenness, limber and light of limb, with hair that looked as if his mother had oiled and brushed it in a glistening lick for the occasion; a lad who walked with a distinctive roll of the shoulders, an utterly captivating swagger like a Cockney errand-boy delivering fish. You could imagine the lively lips pursed to whistle the Lambeth Walk, a tune then much in favour in the metropolitan area; and when in time he began to sport a Middlesex cap which made him look mature and respectable all at once and no longer liable at any unexpected moment to ring the front-door bell and bolt for the corner of the street, he wore it cocked in a sprightly manner over one eye. He batted like a sober-sided elder and he looked like Trabb's boy; and as he found his feet he relaxed the sobriety and disclosed a beautiful unspoiled boyish genius that infected his batsmanship with all the sparkle and scent of a May morning. The last sight I had of Compton before the veils came down was on that last sunny Saturday of the Oval Test of 1939; he did nothing especially memorable, but he walked to the wicket as if he had just got off his bicycle and was going behind the wall for a smoke, and he batted with a shiny well-scrubbed look of cheerful defiance on his face and his England cap stuck slightly sideways on his head; and you hoped that his senior colleagues would see that he washed behind the ears fairly frequently and would look away with a mature indulgence from his habit of flicking inky pellets in the dressing-room. And all the while his feet were eager and restless, and he came down the wicket to the fast bowlers and hit them with short-armed punches here, there and everywhere, and he would go down on flexible knees and sweep the ordinary good-length ball to the right of the square-leg umpire with the utmost impertinence. And he could not have been more individual or attractive; and the war came.

What happened to that endearing boy, that distinctive and Dickensian prodigy, I do not know; for in an extraordinary metamorphosis that I saw paralleled in no other player of any kind, he changed his identity before he appeared again. I heard of him, appearing in Army cricket out and about, in India and elsewhere, and in 1946 I followed at a necessary distance the success of his return to the game. His brilliance was now a thing of no doubt, and his establishment as an England player of authority and even greatness was secure. I rejoiced at this; I still thought of him as my

old friend the Cockney errand-boy with the humorous swagger
and the cheeky happy larking adroitness; grown up of course, but
not much changed; the boy eternal as he was surely cut out to be.
I thought of him with his cap cocked as before, with his hitched
pants and his putative whistle, released from war's alarms and once
more the incarnate truant. Yet when I saw him I barely recognized
him. The boy had gone; missing, perhaps, not killed, as his spirit
inflamed the man Compton to pyrotechnical virtuosities that season
and the next; but hidden and buried, and showing few signs of
return.

The boy Compton had gone; the man Compton was full-faced,
darker than before, broad based, thick in the hips, regular-featured,
even handsome; his hair thick and inclined to fall into his eyes when
over-exerted. The pinkness had left his features, his mischievous
eyes had retreated behind contemplative wrinkles; he was soberer,
firmer set, authoritative, assured. All through the wonderful seasons
when he tore the established records to shreds with some of the most
vigorous and resourceful attacking batting that we had seen since
the early Hammond, I pondered on this curious development; I
could not understand it. The man's very features, the idolized
features which contemplate us from the side of every bus and the
arcades of every underground subway, were different from those
of the lost boy whom I had cherished (as one does) in my own
peculiar possession, with so much peculiar pride. As for his cap,
he wore it no more; I like to think that in a fit of absentmindedness
he lost it.

Luck came and went, his enormous skill was attacked by misfortune, injury unbalanced his gay poise and mobility. He fell,
not on evil days indeed, but upon dark periods of misfortune which
were the worse for the fierce uncompromising ignorance of much
of the publicity he was given and which I doubt if he ever courted.
He lost a fair portion of his youthful innocence, though the story
was that in the days of his greatest success he abated none of his glad
irresponsibility, being as prone as the dunce at the foot of a class
to leave his only shirt in Sheffield or to arrive at a Test match three-
quarters of an hour late. With the grinding of the upper and the
nether millstones of misfortune (though they left him with residual
successes that would have made the reputation of lesser men) a

frown sat between his eyebrows and a middle-aged weight tethered his alert light alacrity to an unaccustomed staidness. Whether his lost youth was among the gaieties he mourned, I do not know.

Yet the man I saw, once again, at Lord's in 1953, under the weary sardonic watchfulness of that old image on the Grand Stand, had summoned to his aid, in a crisis of character and skill, resources of courage that I was delighted to recognize. On another overcast day, under a lightly clouded sky, with the paintwork fresh and neat glimmering palely in the dullness, I saw Compton batting once more, and this time against even more formidable foes than Tate and inexperience. On this very morning, with a superficial appearance of a February afternoon, Compton faced a legion of attackers— a ramping Australian eleven who in the first innings had fired him out for 2 and the rest of the side (a strong M.C.C. team) for a very meagre count; a series of heavy failures in his last Test matches; a vociferous series of erstwhile idolaters hotfoot on his heels to attack; his own shaky self-confidence; an awkward light; and Lindwall.

He faced these attackers and he faced them boldly. In all my experience of him, and I have seen him in my time make quite a large number of runs, I have never felt so pleased and satisfied as he made me feel that morning. The frown still perturbed his brow, and the hair still tumbled over it into his eyes as the energy of his efforts disturbed the commercial beauty of its formal setting; but the art he deployed, physically and psychologically, against this latter-day equivalent of the Seven Deadly Sins aided by Apollyon straddling right across his way, was solid, unruffled, intelligent and ultimately triumphant. He rolled out a clanging glory of an off-drive; he bent to one knee and swept Davidson to the fine-leg boundary; better than all this, he defied the deadly Lindwall for an hour and a half in the teeth of one of the finest and most accurate spells of bowling I have ever seen. Here was a batsman rehabilitated and complete; the loss of some of the glittering *gay savoir* of his sunny prime had been worthily compensated for by this access of responsible maturity, this reliable and watchful competence.

And as I watched I fought, for the most part vainly, to recover from the sturdy frame so admirably performing before me a vestige, a recognizable gesture even, of the young thin pale soft shy slim slip of a thing that so many years before I had sat and watched in that very place. Where had he gone, my delightful urchin? This harassed idol with the weight of his public responsibilities upon him had surely not grown out of the gay whistler of old years? Yet the sober and unavoidable fact remained that he had, and there were moments, there were elusive illuminant moments, when Compton grinned and shoved back his unruly hair, or shook his head as if the flies were at it before he bent to face the bowler (as he had done that other day when he bent to face Tate), when far below the too, too solid flesh I glimpsed the touching struggle for re-emergence of my lost and charming urchin from the other side of the war, from the other side of a barrier of destructiveness, from the other end of a moving and unreturning band of Time. I do not lament, why should I? Time the destroyer is Time the preserver; in Compton there is much of value now that was only present potentially then. Perhaps if I grieve at all it is my own youth I grieve for, feeling that if the primal innocence is going from him, so much the more it must be going from me, who am older than Compton by six years. I take this conspicuous change in one man's aspect as the most striking example I can give of the power to catch, in the context of which I am speaking, the progress of the moment. I have caught Compton's passage in slow motion; it will stand perhaps for the passage of us all.

"It is because they contain the past," wrote Marcel Proust, that great obsessed genius haunted by this preoccupation with Time which visits us all during the course of our lives, "that human bodies can so much hurt those who love them, because they contain so many memories, so many joys and desires effaced within them." This was written of relationships far more intimate and intense than that I speak of now; it is far from my thoughts or intentions to saddle an unpretentious cricketer with emotional ramifications of this kind. But lighten Proust's reference a little and you can see what I mean; and you can see how the spectacle of cricket as it passes before me, slowly but with a remorseless inevitability, can produce at times an awful warmth about my heart like a load of mortality. Hobbs passed and Hammond passed, but this is worse still. For Compton has not passed yet, and I hope it will be very many years before he does; yet even his unfinished passage is fraught with implications of its end. I cannot go to see Compton in 1956 and still think it is 1936. That the clock can stop at all is an illusion.

Francis Thompson knew this, and stayed away from Lord's. He had anchored himself passionately in the moment, the moment of Hornby and Barlow, and when they passed from the scene they took with them the mainspring of his interest in the game. For him, perhaps, the game was not intrinsically interesting or very important; its value to him was the expression of its vitality in the persons of certain lively and entertaining characters, and he had no sustaining desire to transfer their functions to new models when once they were no longer there to act in their own persons. A part of Thompson's youth clove to Hornby and Barlow, and he was not sufficiently dispassionate (and I will not blame him) to be able to mark off with stoic detachment the disappearance of the moment he had loved. His life had not been happy, and I surmise that Hornby and Barlow signified to him a lost loveliness far more poignant than, say, Hobbs and Sandham could ever have signified for myself, infinitely less plagued by fortune than Thompson. It would take considerably more than the absence of Hobbs and Sandham to keep me away from the Oval; but I could not presume to dispute with a poet like Thompson on the necessity of such a self-abnegation as he practised. It wrote for him a lyric that in places touches the heart to tears; I can never read it without sensing an early misty grey morning at Lord's in the twenties, when the ground really did seem ghostly, and where the crowd did really seem to be clapping without sound the flickering figures of the cricketers, Hendren and Hearne as I recall; when I read Thompson's lyric it is of them that I naturally think, and I all but weep with the geniune universal sadness whose springs he has for once and for the moment succeeded in tapping. " It is because they contain the past" —Proust's voice is melancholy and insistent and finally persuasive— " that human bodies can so much hurt those who love them, because they contain so many memories." Thompson did not *love* Hornby and Barlow; I did not *love* Hobbs or Sandham or Hammond or Compton, Heaven forbid; but there were tight emotional relationships between us, the spectators, and these cricketers, or should I say the idea of these cricketers; and since when Proust says " love " he may generally be regarded as meaning " enter into an emotional relationship with," then we can accept his remark as applying closely to our common plight. Francis Thompson and I, and no doubt a hundred thousand others, know the pain of the evanescence of our youth, as perceived in the passing of the cricketers we once knew and worshipped.

It is a curious parallelism, the unwinding of the history of cricket and the unwinding of the history of our own lives. For most people there is no serious point of contact between the two, and why should there be? One's life is one's life, one's cricket, whether played or watched, is one's relaxation. Very good; and the long bannered progress of the great cricketers across the scene of the game is only a publicization of a pastime, like recurrent comic strips or television serials. I suppose that may be said to be true in a sense. No wonder then that the parallel lines do not meet.

I am not going to insist on geometrical analogies; upon which my touch is tentative at the best. But there are, I am convinced, some people on the progress of whose emotional lives this bright stream of artificial activity has from time to time impinged. As I have already stated, implicitly and explicitly, cricket has provided for me perhaps the most poignant symbols I have known of the passage of time. It has done more than suggest a convenient allegorical illustration; it has itself supplied the original emotive point from which my imagination has begun to work. More than that (though in a sense, perhaps, not quite so much as that), it has lent to moments of emotional or nervous difficulty emblems of serenity that I could not, in those given circumstances, have done without. In periods of temperamental, and I am glad to say temporary, distraction it has been of genuinely sedative importance to me that, notwithstanding such emotional circumstances as for the moment conspired to confuse me, Hutton or Hammond, or whoever I chanced to think of, was even at that moment beautifully and impersonally batting in the sunshine, going through the predetermined motions of a deliciously impersonal game.

One such instance I have briefly referred to already. When I was twelve I went for the first time to see the Champion County match at the Oval right at the autumnal finish of the season. It was an annual festival that I was sorry to see discontinued; it gave us on

the depressing fringe of football a last sad view of our old friends—
usually a near-England side—and it provided, more often than not,
cracking good spectacle. We schoolboys loved it; I doubt at this
end of the perspective of time whether the cricketers themselves
were over-keen on it, coming as it did at the end of an exhausting
season when they all felt no doubt that they had had enough. The
exhilarating cricket that we so often saw was probably relaxed
country stuff to them; which accounts for my memories of two of
the fiercest bouts of hitting that I ever remember seeing—one by
Hendren and Ames at the expense of Hopwood and Iddon of
Lancashire, and the other, the one I am thinking most particularly
of, by Woolley and Chapman on this bright September day when
I was twelve.

Fortune favoured the two left-handers on that day; and, I have
since thought, a relaxed carelessness on the part of the two bowlers,
Rhodes and Kilner, whom in normal conditions no one hit with
impunity. But the Fates were with the batsmen, and it was the
last game of the season, and it was a lovely bright day (September
15th, 1924, I shall remember the date all my life) and the bowlers'
fingers were perhaps September-weary, and the left-hander's
spinner to the left-handed batsmen encouraged a gladsome sweep
to leg with the break—and altogether we were presented with such
conditions as never before or since concatenated so gloriously;
and these two beautiful left-handers, Woolley in a roseate dream of
willowy motion and Chapman in a great muscular charging flourish
of strong limbs in their pride, collected fifty runs off these tremendous bowlers in exactly seven minutes by the clock. Woolley's right
foot, again and again, planted itself lengthily down the wicket
as he swung lazily with the break; Chapman, all of him, came
swinging out in delight with his bat flourishing high—and time and
again the ball soared splendidly over the crowd, out into the road,
under the gasometer. I can still hear the joyous crack, still rise with
the excited crowd around me as the ball sails above our heads,
join in the high squall of delighted cheering, wave on wave of it,
and down comes Chapman again and crack comes the ball once
more into our midst. I felt, innocent and inexperienced as I was,
a sense of tremendous exultation. It was elementary, charity-match
stuff; but it affected me as no incident at any cricket match has ever

affected me, before or since. For the rest of the day I felt breathless, dizzy, almost ill ; the ordinary world seemed unreal. But for years later, literally years, the memory of those moments (which Woolley and Chapman have probably forgotten; I doubt whether I can say the same of Rhodes) recurred to me and, curiously enough, steadied me at times when steadying was what I most needed. Being blessed with more than usually good health, I naturally when I feel off-colour for a few hours imagine that I am going to die; and on many of these not very frequent but not unknown occasions during adolescence and later, whenever I woke up in the night visited by such fears as often plague our humanity for very little cause, I would find my palpitations quietened almost inevitably by a handhold out of the past from that bright little incident of my boyhood. The sunny Oval, and Chapman, all red-faced and laughing, dancing out to drive, and the ball soaring and the crowd rising and cheering, made a living light-giving cameo that very many times in the lonely night-watches of real or imaginary distress cooled and soothed my agitation and eased me into a quieter mood of resignation or sleep. It is a part of the past that is bodily of the present still.

Other occasions there were too, when a cricket match, for one adventitious reason or another, reached across into the domains of my life and took its place there for good or ill. For one horrifying chilly afternoon, on the day before the result of my Finals at the Bar examinations was announced, I sat hunched and quivering and gnawing my knuckles and my umbrella in a semi-deserted Oval pavilion while a perverse Gloucestershire, a team of all the talents, played Surrey to a fruitless draw when all they had to do was to go for an adventurous crack and win, saving my gibbering soul from its twenty-four-hour perdition the while. They had Barnett, Hammond, Dacre, B. H. Lyon—what more could they ask? I suppose if in addition they had had W. G. Grace and Jessop they would have tried; but as it was they prodded and poked and increased my sour sense of damnation into a state of near suicidal gloom. Barnett was out before I came; Hammond played the most constipated innings I ever saw him play; Dacre and Lyon took their cues from him and the match dribbled and watered away until I got up and slumped out in misery. I found next day that I had passed; but no thanks were due to Gloucestershire. The dead tree gave no shelter, the cricket no relief.

Many years later I sat for another Final examination, for an external university degree, and awaited the result at Hastings during a very hot and run-swollen cricket week. Something went wrong with my communication system and as it turned out I had to get back to London before I ever found out my result; and the last few days of the week were spent in a knotted tangle of wrought-up nerves that to recall is purgatory and to describe would be hell. Laying a quiet and relaxing hand across my turmoil is the memory of a long hot day when Sussex played Leicester; and as the nightmare of waiting was crowned happily enough with a rather gratifying and unsuspected measure of success, I never now think of that sun-baked day and of the men who moved through it without investing them, Harry Parks and James Langridge in particular, for they each scored a hundred, with a touch of the pleasure and joy that awaited me at the end of the few hot harrowing days of doubt.

One other memory I have, and Sussex has again a special place in it, though this time it is an earlier Sussex, the Sussex of the salt Brighton air which tanged their cricket so attractively in the twenties and early thirties. This time I was caught in a very susceptible emotional condition indeed; for on the morning when I travelled to Hove to see Sussex play Gloucestershire I had received for the very first time a letter from the girl who not many years later became my wife. It was in no accepted sense of the word a love letter; it was a response merely to some terribly nervous and no doubt clumsy and inexperienced overture of mine. It was 1933, I was twenty, I had been overtaken unawares by a tumult of sensations that I hardly began to understand, I had gone down before it irreclaimably in love. The letter in my pocket, friendly and restrained in terms, might have been, to my then inflated sensitivity, written by Cleopatra to Antony. It burned in my pocket all day, I took it out and read it no doubt at the fall of each wicket, I pored over it until even before the drawing of stumps it began to come apart at the folds. Because of that letter the cricket I saw on that day is graven in my memory as if on gold. It was oven-hot but for the light breeze off the sea; and off an attack weakened by Goddard's

absence, Sussex collected over 500 runs. Charlie Parker's graceful
action spun unremittingly from one end; Sinfield, Barnett,
Hammond strove from the other. It was no good. Bowley got
runs, the Parks brothers got runs, the lean elegant James Langridge
got runs, and Cook made over 160. It was an orgiastic day and the
Gloucestershire fielders ran like melted butter. Towards the end
when they had an hour's batting, the astonishing Barnett made 53
in an hour, an entrancing performance which effectively prevented
me from seeing Hammond bat, which I had come all the way to
Brighton especially to do. But I had had God's plenty; and I read
the letter again in a contented haze of relaxed satisfaction, incor-
porating there and then into my private world of happiness the
brothers Parks and the brothers Langridge, Maurice Tate and Tom
Cook, Charlie Parker and Charlie Barnett, and of course Hammond.
(I was glad that he was there; it added a fitting dimension to my
appreciation.) Whether my wife suspects—she probably does—
that in some sort she has shared the inner mysteries of a man's
imagination and emotional responses with these honest men whom
she has never seen; whether she suspects it or whether she approves
it, I do not know. I know well enough that she will be charitable
and count it no harm. She is still here; nearly all the players from
that dazzling day are gone from the scene—all but John Langridge,
and with respect to a worthy cricketer, my wife is hardly likely to
find him a serious rival to her in my affections. They are nearly
all gone; their moment, in cricket and in Time, has been marked
off into the past; but because their moment, though they could not
have known it, enriched for ever a moment of my own that was
already of unusual warrant and price in my life, then that moment
in Time has been, and can always be, carried from the past into
the present, and from there indefinitely into the future. The clock
will not stop, I know; Father Time, swinging sardonically over
Lord's, still bends to the removal of the fatal bail; but there are
moments that can cheat the clock and can cheat Time. For a
moment or two, at any rate; and here below that is all we can ask
or need.

CHAPTER NINE

BANSTEAD CRICKET

If I stand and look through the gap in the rather untidy hedge at the bottom of my garden I can see the low red-tiled roof of the cricket pavilion squatting between its tall white flagpoles. Between the garden hedge and the cricket ground is a wide field with a right of way running through the middle of it; this field is a mass of buttercups in May, and is crowded with cows or their traces all the year round. The right of way leads from the straggling houses of the little hamlet half a mile off among the trees, direct to the centre of Banstead village. If you come from the hamlet, which sports a notable public-house, and take the path across the cowfield among (at the right time of year) the buttercups, and keep along a line set you by the tall spire of Banstead church, you will proceed arrow-sure diagonally across the cricket ground, passing in front of deepish mid-off and normal extra cover and crossing perhaps just behind cover-point's back. You need feel no compunction in doing this, as there is an unalienable public right of way slap-bang across the square, and if any dogged citizen with no regard for the niceties and politenesses of the game cares to avail himself (or more often, herself) of the public privilege, then there is nothing that the Chairman of the Council or the President of the M.C.C. can do about it. Many is the time that I have put my hands in my pockets in the slips and whistled while some indifferent old cottager, laden with string bags, packets of breakfast cereals and detergents, and fourteen pounds of potatoes, waddled back home from the Saturday afternoon shopping oblivious of the whistles and the handclaps and the ostentatious clearings of the throat that never fail to accompany this perilous North-West passage which I would rather die than navigate myself.

Banstead cricket ground lies in a level landscape, close against the busy village on the one side, open to gently declining pastureland on the other. Going in to bat at the end opposite the village, you look past the bowler at a magnificent row of limes, twelve of them, spaced grandly out between extremely deep long-on in the left-hand far corner and impossibly deep extra cover with his heels on the boundary to the far right. Look round the off-side field in a meditative way, deciding whether or not it's worth while trying for a short single to cover to get off the mark, and the breadth of your vision will be restricted and your whole imagination dwarfed by an even more magnificent row of chestnuts (twelve of them too) heavy laden in the main summer months with the opulent candle-blossom in pink and white and the grand green weight of their enormous leaves. All round the ground, varying in numbers according to the weather or the occasion, sit the spectators in their deck-chairs, in their cars, on their benches, on the grass; a gathering from which you could compile a reasonably representative Who's Who in Banstead, vicar and verger, publican and plumber, school-master, ratepayer, beggarman and thief, with wives and families to match, as integral a part of the scene as the cricketers themselves and as essential to the life in the landscape. The pavilion sits demurely away at square-leg; lounging out in front of that pavilion on the seats behind the clipped box-hedge, summer after summer, I have seen the cricket dwarf itself, be reduced to the old ritual again, to the æsthetic motions and no more, before the backcloth of these overwhelming trees. The hawthorn blossoms at Tansonville, the lilacs on the Méséglise Way, were not more precious or more revealing to the young Marcel than the chestnut blossoms to the Banstead cricketer who has watched on the patch of green between him and them a whole generation of Banstead players come and flourish and pass. Standing at the wicket, though, facing the sight-screen shaded by the straggling lime-leaves, you are conscious of protection, of the dark limes cutting out the bustle and traffic of the village, the tennis courts and the children on the swings, the buses and the bowling green and the north wind blowing over London; of the darker and heavier chestnuts ramparting the highest breath of the easterly gales. Banstead is a high village and a cold one; from certain points on its tableland the eye can travel to the Thames Valley, to Harrow-on-the-Hill, to the Hampstead heights, to the back door of the North Downs and to the gates of Kent; and in May and September, not to speak of the months in between, the chestnuts and the limes round the cricket field perform a grateful protective function, giving serenity, illusory perhaps but effective, from the fiercer of the customary winds.

Take a quick single and face the bowling from the other end and you are in a different world. You are engulfed in light; from deep long-on to deeper extra cover this time there seems barely a may bush and a holly tree between you and eternity. From your feet the green grass flows outwards to the low hedge beyond the critical and strategic deck-chairs, and for all you know thereafter it stops altogether. Facing the village you feel sheltered against the world; facing the other way you might but for the may and the holly and the comforting tops of a few clusters of elms be falling over its very edge. Light comes in at you like an invasion; backed by the prevailing south-west, the clouds sail in incessantly season after season after their great processional voyage up the English Channel, heavy with Atlantic evaporation. Sometimes we receive this latter in heavy rain; quite often not. During the day the sun goes over diagonally like the right of way, making piously for the church spire; the field gets the whole blazing wash of it from morning till evening, as the limes and the chestnuts are so placed that they retard the wind and receive the light. It is never at eye-level until late evening or, in September, late afternoon, when it slopes behind the church in streaming red fire and flings the lime-shadows from the far long-on corner as far as close mid-wicket; and batsmen facing the village end tug their caps over their left eyes, and it is good policy to try a high donkey drop on or outside the leg stump which may or may not get clouted for four, but, whatever its intrinsic fate, will oblige the unwary batsman to look straight into the blaze.

Banstead is nominally a village, though some doubt whether in these suburban times it can seriously retain that distinction. I think it just succeeds, mainly by virtue of its separation from the spreading stain of outer London by the width of the virtually impassable Banstead Downs. It is a matter of fascinating local history that these, and many thousand beautiful acres of open space, were preserved for us in the teeth of ruthless capitalist exploitation by the efforts of one John Robertson, a leading member of the Banstead Cricket Club, who sustained for more than ten years the strain and expense of a heartbreaking lawsuit which finally, against all probability, succeeded in rescuing from the builder an area of downland which has affected all our lives. Standing in the slips as the bowler runs up from the village end you can see glimpses of a High Street over-lavish with its concrete and sham oak timber, its chain stores and its Woolworth's—a High Street that even in my lifetime was a gravelly road between high banks, with another row of limes where Tesco and the Co-op and Boots and the radio shops now stand—limes between whose stems you could follow with the eye where the ground fell sharply from your feet in a slowly levelling slope that did not end until you were among the chimneys and masts of London river fifteen miles away.

So Banstead was once a village, and even if the illusion has gone from its High Street and its proliferation of housing estates it dies very hard indeed in the green corner between the limes and the chestnuts. The ground itself is known generally as the Green (" up on the Green ") by players and members, and not by its official and unsuggestive title of " the Avenue Road Cricket Ground." This affectionate generality preserves the village atmosphere whether intentionally or not; and so does the view from the village end, with its pastoral spaciousness, its low holly hedges, its glimpsed vistas of straying browsing cows in the adjoining fields, its distant elms and distant glint of sunlight on the whitewashed walls of cottages. A country cricket ground surrounded by farms and quiet houses, set in a village which is still a village, even if only tenuously so. The quality of the cricket might be expected to correspond.

Village cricket, as such, has been fed to the public consciousness for so long now that it has solidified in the common imagination as an unchangeable and slightly patronizable element in our social life. Serious writers like Sassoon and Blunden, humorous writers like Macdonell and a host of anonymities in the comic weeklies, coupled with the light-fingered chatter of music-hall and radio, have built up in the Englishman's mind a delicious feudal pastoral played out in the shadows of church spire and inn sign amid sporadic interruption from dogs and boys; in which the Vicar plays, classically but ineffectively, and the Squire plays, farcically but ineffectively, but the central figure of all, as imperatively necessary as Harlequin in the harlequinade, is inevitably the village blacksmith, wearing a collarless shirt, black trousers and braces (inescapable braces), who, with less technique than anyone, deals more destruction than all his colleagues put together, who breaks stumps with the fury of his indiscriminate fast bowling and hits Gargantuan sixes with his eyes tight shut.

Village cricket as played on Banstead village cricket green is not of this kind at all. Banstead appreciates its rural setting without in any way mistaking it for a rustic one; the quality of its cricket is as rural as may be, but (with a few glaring exceptions over whom heads are shaken) is not rustic at all. If the village possessed a village blacksmith, and if the village blacksmith were a cricketer, he would be welcomed with rejoicing in the cricket club whether he wore braces or not, but he would be discouraged from putting on a professional funny act and he would be expected to look at the ball before hitting it, or trying to hit it, into the top branches of the lime trees. It occurs to me at the moment of writing that we in the cricket club require to know so little about each other, apart from whether we prefer to bowl into the wind or with it or whether we possess a car useful for away matches, that it is quite possible that I have been playing for half a dozen seasons with the village blacksmith on the same side without being aware of it. He may be any one of half a dozen well-turned-out and affable colleagues of mine whose professions I do not know without asking point-blank, which I am disinclined to do in case I put them to the embarrassment of confessing something dishonourable, like an author or a Government official; he may, on the other hand, be a non-playing member, possibly even a vice-president. I do not greatly care; we are all equal in the sight of God, especially when the sun is low over the church spire and the lime shadows are tricky. Our eccentricities are in our characters and not in our trades.

Banstead Cricket Club is well over a hundred years old, and I gather that it was preserved for nearly all that time as a kind of gentlemen's village team—a wealthy set of squires, landowners and gentry amusing themselves with lavish gentility with the help of a gaggle of impressed men from among the tenantry and artisan population of the surrounding fields and farmsteads. Preserved for more than two generations in the personnel of the club like an indestructible fly in amber was a venerable relic of those delightfully illiberal days—the famous George Muggeridge. This astonishing character joined the club in 1904 at the beck and call, no doubt, of those among the gentry who employed him during the week as odd-job man-of-all-work, builder, decorator, gardener and what-they-willed. He possessed then, I am told, as he possessed to his dying day, a pair of piercing eyes that looked at you past a formidable long nose, and a leathery face in which as he smiled (which he did sardonically when getting the better of someone or other) his moustache went up under his nose and his nose came down over his moustache like the villain in *Little Dorrit*. He was gifted with a cavalier unorthodoxy in his style of batting, which is said to have brought him in all twenty-one centuries; since I knew him, and I knew him twenty years, I never saw him bat higher than Number 9, so much of this to me is legendary, not to say prehistoric. Age and cunning had twisted his maturing body into a kind of watchful crouch, from which he still moved off in the summer before his death with clockwork inevitability every Saturday afternoon to bowl (if he could possibly arrange it) the first ball of the innings. He slung down a very tricky medium-paced ball from what was virtually a round-arm action; it moved wickedly across the batsman's legs and it preserved a deadly accuracy. He bowled along these lines for over fifty years; he loved bowling and hated the over when he had to wait his turn while his colleague bowled from the other end. By sheer force of accuracy and attrition he collected scores of wickets, and champed and chafed when anyone else bagged a batsman he had marked down as his own. (This usually meant a whole side, so other bowlers had to look out for grumbles.) I stood in the slips once as the bowler ran up to bowl the first ball in the first match of the season. George, who was to bowl the second over, was next to me at second slip. When the first ball beat the unfortunate batsman and whipped his off stump out of the ground, George gave vent to a sort of coughing grunt, whether of delight or of extreme chagrin it was impossible to determine. " Spoilt George's afternoon," I observed to Jock Rignall, our admirably solid captain-wicket-keeper as he fitted the stump back. " Spoilt his afternoon?" sniggered Jock behind his gloves, "spoilt his whole bloody season."

But it didn't, you know; George, who at the time was, I believe, about sixty-four, bowled with intense enthusiasm and pertinacity until one day going about his normal and lawful occasions he fell off a ladder and hurt his leg; he stood down with infuriated reluctance for one week and arrived back on the following Saturday like a youth of sixteen let out of school. With a ferocious glint in his hawk-like eyes he took 9 for 24 that day; in triumph he swept away the last few paltry batsmen, laughed to the skies with his moustache going up and his nose coming down, and replied to the congratulations with the following classic utterance—"There ain't none o' you other buggers can't get no bloody wickets."

Admirable George Muggeridge, half as old as Time and twice as wily; when I joined the club twenty years ago he was barely fifty and looked sixty-five; in the long procession of the years he turned sixty-five and looked barely fifty, an oracular pertinacious figure looking like the late Mahatma Gandhi in a cricket cap, gnarled, cross-grained, friendly and apparently permanent. A Surrey man who might temperamentally have been born and bred in Yorkshire, he rivalled Wilfred Rhodes and Emmott Robinson in his supreme confidence in his own destructive powers, and had quite as much justification as they. He bowled, indispensably, for the 1st XI until after the Second World War, then he dropped to the second, and later to the higher of the two thirds (IIIa), where I coincided with him for two or three happy seasons before wavering up into the second, where I have my precarious home. But I still heard tales of old George bowling unchanged on afternoons of crushing heat, of sheaves of wickets and explosive rumblings in the slips, of crowing delighted laughter as yet another batsman got his legs in front of one that did not rise. Not long ago the appreciative club made him a life member; but after all it could only supply a formal and barely necessary endorsement to a fact which he had himself created. He might have bowled for Banstead under Queen Victoria; he would have been unusually young, but he might have. He did in fact bowl for Banstead under Queen Elizabeth; he was unusually old, but he did. George Muggeridge piloted Banstead through its own era of social change, which

faintly and generally reflects the far more violent and fundamental
social changes in the big world beyond the chestnuts and the limes.
He began by being humble before the club; at the end the club was,
in a sense, humble before him. He was all that remained of the old
village green team; and I would rather have faced, even in George's
last summer, the village blacksmith in his braces. Death took him,
cleanly and quickly, in the winter; George Muggeridge never
retired.

I joined Banstead in 1932, a green youth fresh from the naïve
authoritarianism of a school 1st XI, to plunge for virtually the first
time into the far easier and less emulatory world of club cricket.
The undemanding friendliness took me aback at first, accustomed
as I was to an almost Spartan rigour. In my hypersensitive state I
felt it took the edge off the cricket; but I know quite well that it
performed the far more salutary duty of taking the edge off me.
By this time, of course, the club had long sloughed off all traces
(except George Muggeridge) of its feudal origin and was taking
substantial colour from the growing resemblance of the parent
village to an outlying suburb; it had split its original single team
into a regular two and a very fairly regular third (these, reinforced
by a fourth, which to bolster its *amour propre* is called IIIb, are
functioning at high pressure nowadays from one end of the season
to the other). The qualities and comparative qualities of these sides
are not particularly steep; I have known one man, with no particular incongruity, represent in one season both IIIb and the 1st XI;
the same season in which another man, with no incongruity whatever, represented both the 1st XI and the Players at Lord's. At
Banstead we span the heights and the depths with equanimity,
and are placidly at home with either. All sorts and conditions of
characters find equal welcome; although I take it that usually most
of us (being civil servants, accountants, insurance officials, heads of
small businesses and the like) are just a cross-section of black-coated
officialdom, we do sport sprinklings of other less tediously monotonous professions. We had a bookmaker who was a sterling opening
batsman and no mean left-arm spinner; I played for some years
with a lad who was actually a tea-taster and who naturally never
touched the stuff they dished us out in cups between the innings;
one of my recent captains makes a living, and it looks a very good

one too, supervising the cleaning of windows belonging to citizens who are barely fit to clean his boots. We in the club who are in Government departments vie tacitly with one another to give the firmest impression of mystery and importance. To wear an Anthony Eden hat to a match and to accompany it with a brief-case and a neatly rolled umbrella; to give club officials an office telephone number which will necessitate your being approached through three separate secretaries and confidential clerks; or to reveal in the course of casual bar conversation that since the game on the previous Saturday you have flown to Washington and back on urgent Cabinet business—all this is common form and we all rival our colleagues in establishing for ourselves an aloof and impressive *cachet* which is designed to make our fellow cricketers whisper behind their hands—as a counterblast to the prevailing impression that we spend half the summer at inter-departmental cricket matches and the other half at the Oval. But much of this is by the way, and in the bar or the dressing-room or the slips nobody cares how important or unimportant his fellow's public life may be; all that is demanded is that he shall pay his round at the first, refrain from poaching pegs in the second and hold a reasonable number of catches in the third. When I first joined in 1932 I was received as myself; so I am in 1955, with the difference that they were polite then, but see no further necessity for it now. I would not have it otherwise.

When I joined I was shy and keen, fielded much in the country under the limes, batted late in the order, fetched and carried and absorbed new places and faces with avidity. I came to the club at its last stage of transition when the old feudalities were dying; the captain, Tom Norris, an old Carthusian who had just missed an Oxford Blue, and was by this time I suppose in his early fifties, was of the grand seigneur type, ever affable but ever aloof. With me he kept his kindness and kept his distance; his warmth, which was genuine and spontaneous, was too subtle for my inexperience. I responded more to his vice-captain Stanley Baker, a fast-medium bowler with a glorious high action and a captivating twinkle, everybody's friend and now in this late time president, who would if need arose submit himself to be rolled into the pitch with the heavy roller for the club's sake; to Bob Ward, at that time the most enthusiastic club cricketer I had ever met, with an eager anxious lined face that put years on his youth and a terrier's intentness on the job in hand, be it batting, bowling or fielding, all of which he did uncommonly well with a positively frightening expenditure of nervous energy; and last but foremost, to the great Bill Smith, a cricketer of beautiful proportions and performance, the spectator's joy. Always at the fall of the first wicket Bill Smith would emerge from the pavilion, powerful and broad-shouldered, moving easily and lightly, putting on his gloves. He was not a classical player but he was the most devastating club batsman I have seen; his feet were not always planted right, and he flailed at the good-length balls with a cross bat; but a short ball on the off to Bill Smith was four runs before cover had regained his equilibrium, and any-thing over-pitched was hit with stunning violence anywhere between extra-cover and mid-wicket. It was a horrible experience to be in with him; one of his favourite reactions was a most fearful belt off the middle and off stumps which went past the bowler at head-height just about where the non-striker would normally be standing; on many occasions I have been constrained to throw myself flat before this whistling onslaught, which, being spon-taneous and entirely unscientific, was also unexpected. His bat sounded as rich as a great gong, and he hit a disproportionate number of sixes slap off the middle of it; and once, I inconsequently remember, he hit an extraordinary cross-batted sweep first ball with it, off either the middle or the off-stump, which rose in a whooshing arc behind square-leg and was grandly caught by a deep fielder in front of the pavilion flagstaff, going all out. Bill no doubt accepted this, as he accepted his more customary successes, with an equable cheerfulness that was part of a convivial and friendly disposition; and compensated with several spells of energetic bowl-ing and alert slip fielding. In later years he became captain; and even before that time I came to regard him as a kind of father-figure in the team, legendary in the club's history and the cause of hysteria among the younger spectators. Quietly and unobtrusively he did me many small kindnesses; when Norris, doubtless for some good reason, dropped me from Number 7 to Number 10, it was Bill Smith who came to me where I brooded in silence and slipped a timely word of encouragement into my private mystification. It was Bill Smith who sent a telegram when I got married and Bill Smith who showed most interest when I began to publish novels (though I doubt if he ever got so far as to read them). He played cricket with a genial and effective adventurousness, and enjoyed its companionable delights. Once he completed his 1,000 runs for the season in the last match; he had spent the morning nerving himself for the ordeal in the most practical way that occurred to him, and although he scraped the necessary few runs it was a damned close-run thing, and he spent the rest of that most remarkable and memorable day giggling incongruously in the slips. Since he gave up, health and circumstances have been less than kind to him; but I remember him as, unconsciously, the prime agent of my own cricketing maturity.

He it was who had the most soothing word in the humorous tumult that arose in the early days when I was caught reading Swinburne in the dressing-room. A salutary experience for a precocious and priggish adolescent, for I was little more ; " Reads *The Hymn to Proserpine* and wears braces like this! " shouted one humorist, waving a pair of natty articles I much prized embroidered with hearts, clubs, spades and diamonds; Bill led a moderate form of opposition and the hue and cry died away—except that Stanley Baker has occasionally referred to me in later years as " old Poetry," a collocution that charms me utterly—and nothing of the tumult remained but Len Cole nodding sagely to himself in the corner, saying to whoever cared to listen, " Don't you have anything to do with it. It's all moonshine, that's what it is, it's all moonshine."

Len Cole's wide-eyed rubbery face is present in all my dreams of Banstead, waking or sleeping. He resembles (he will forgive me) a rabbit made up as a clown, or a clown made up as a rabbit; his pliant physiognomy, very happily reminiscent of Harpo Marx, exudes a perky independence of spirit that is an everlasting delight to contemplate. Bill Smith was the most devastating club batsman I have seen; Len Cole was by far the best. At the wicket the rabbit and the clown vanished, his jaw projected as he hunched himself, his eyes lost their vivacity and glared ruthlessly down the pitch. He was a product of Mitcham, a famous forcing-house of Surrey talent, when I first encountered him long before I ever played for Banstead, when he in his very early youth scored a brilliant hundred against a wandering side I was assisting on Mitcham's cricket green, until the packed Bank Holiday crowd was vociferating " Well played, Coley boy! " to drown the buses and trams. He brought a seasoned, almost professional skill out of Mitcham to leaven the congenial ruralities of Banstead; and I know of nothing to calm the nervous tremors at the start of an innings more than the sight of Len Cole reflectively chewing gum at the wicket, scowling contemptuously at the bowler, who is as likely as not one of his oldest friends, making his cool precise shot with about thirty seconds more to spare than seems humanly possible, and walking the easy single, still chewing. For twenty seasons he has rioted among runs, a compact busy stylist with all the strokes, including a mule's kick of a hook, and half the afternoon to play them in. He has more age and weight than he or anyone else would wish now, but he has perennial quality and would stare defiance in the eyes of Lindwall himself; he still moves lightly into the easy economical poise that is the sign of the batsman born, he still infects his less experienced colleagues at the other end with at least a fraction of his God-given confidence. As far as I am concerned, while Banstead still has her Len, England is welcome to hers.

Once freed of the concentrations of batsmanship, Len relaxes in the field, slower than he was but safe for a snap catch even yet. As long as he is near enough for a brisk and absorbing chat with the next fielder or the batsman he will be happy; since he is prouder of his wit than of his batting skill, ignoring the relative valuations placed on these commodities by his friends. He honours me and the bystanders with a perennial reminiscence about myself and a certain match against Beddington which I am sure is inaccurate and which I will not bother to transcribe; and with the talismanic repetition of a joke about a parrot which confused the village idiot by addressing him in English. Len Cole never fails when meeting me casually in the street, or even, on occasions, in the middle of the pitch, to raise his hat (or in the latter case, his cap) and compressing his pliable features into the nearest possible semblance of complete vacuity, to say whimsically, " Sorry, sir; I thought you wuz a bird." As a corollary to which it may be useful to recall, as he himself will do, that on the first occasion when he, reputation and all, first took the field for Banstead, his captain, Stanley Baker, pointed to the far corner of the field and said " Deep third man, you; and deep long-on when the bowling's this end. There," turning to the rest of the dispersing eleven, " that's got rid of him for the afternoon. No more of his bloody chatter till tea-time."

Len Cole's rich and prolific batsmanship took over from Bill Smith and piloted Banstead cricket through the thirties and forties with immense success. He was one of the symbols of continuity that I most welcomed when I returned to Banstead myself, after an eight-year gap, in 1947. Much had gone but much abode, and abode with honour and energy. Only two or three years back, on a Saturday when I was not playing, I took some visitors into the cricket field through the stile in the cow-meadow. It was a superb hot day in early June; the limes and the chestnuts alike were green, protective, productive, reassuring. The bowlers sweated like Falstaff, the fielders were scattered like the hosts of Sennacherib. Banstead 210 for 1, read the scoreboard; and there in the middle was Len Cole, his face bright beetroot, a sweat-rag round his neck, his running between the wickets a painful affair of laggard steps, but his stroke-play, for certainty and punishment-power, a joy. He made over 100 that day; and so too did his second-wicket part-ner, his successor in the great hierarchy of Banstead batting, Jerry Bush.

Jerry Bush is, like myself, a Government official; he is one of the most eminent of Civil Service representative cricketers. Tall, lean, serious, an athlete's mind in an athlete's body, Jerry Bush brings a frowning concentration to his play that even Len Cole, with his residuum of puckish irreverence, cannot command. There is nothing puckish or irreverent about Jerry; he keeps his affability and humour for off the field. He bends the considerable forces of staid mind and flexible body to bear squarely upon this game, and has resulted in becoming one of the best-feared batsmen in London club cricket. He scores prodigiously in departmental and repre-sentative matches; he scores prodigiously for Banstead. He bowls cleverly, slow spinners well flighted, and is a highly capable fielder. The only way to tie him down at the wicket is to bowl a length on his off-stump; the right hander's normal weakness, on the line of his legs, is no weakness at all to him, who is as impervious as rock on that side of the wicket. He can deal anything on the leg stump a crushing, stunning clout all along the ground, wherever the ball pitches or at whatever pace it arrives. Len is perhaps the more finished player of the two, or was; Jerry nowadays commands a crisper and more inevitable execution. I wish I could have seen them bat together when I met them first, in 1933, when Jerry was not yet twenty and already a world's wonder, and Len a robust twenty-eight or so and at the height of his powers. But Jerry did not come to Banstead until well after the war; and by that time Len's reduction by age had already begun.

I missed the war period, which was the time of the first cricket engendering of the Pratt brothers and Dave Fletcher, who went to Surrey with such *réclame*. That little hiatus robbed me of the pleasure of being in at the birth, and when they come back from time to time I am not of the Banstead they know and recognize, though I was playing Banstead cricket while they were toddling. Their rise heralded the new Banstead into which I returned; I found it took me time to settle down, I failed to find form or security for a while and at one point nearly gave up in despair, but ultimately found two havens of refuge—the IIIa XI under Jock Rignall, or the 2nd XI under my old friend Bob Ward.

The cricket in IIIa is mixed and various, involves many congenial characters as well as Banstead's very congenial tree-lined second ground on the outskirts of the village, and brought me a happy season or two when I wanted encouragement and got it. I began to enjoy opening the innings, my partner being the optimistic and eupeptic Malcolm Russell, a very good left-hander some classes below his deserts; he piloted me genially to a few good scores and at least one century partnership on a broiling afternoon. Going in with Malcolm one August Bank Holiday Saturday, I most surprisingly made my first century; Malcolm saw me to the first fifty before he went, and my good colleagues (and the five fielders who dropped me) did all in my support that could be required. I nearly collapsed with exhaustion several times; when, eventually, I made the agricultural hoick which brought me what wild horses would not persuade me ever to describe as a " ton," I was assailed with felicitations by all my very generous opponents. " I suppose you've made lots of these before? " inquired mid-on, shaking my sopping batting-glove. " No, I haven't," I gasped, " it's my first, and now

I can die happy. And as a matter of fact I think I'm going to die now."

Since that time I have enjoyed excursions up and down the elevens, and I have for the moment come to rest in the second. This side, after rather erratic fortunes, had come in 1949 under the captaincy of Bob Ward, and had suddenly coagulated into a living organism of real vitality and character. Assisted by the new captain's apparently unbalanced obsession for letting the other side have first knock, the first full season under his control provided at least six photo-finishes, including one excoriating tie with Mitcham, when our last man was given out l.b.w. with the fifth ball of the last over. Batsmen under Bob's benign influence flowered into stylists, the bowlers bowled at the wickets and hit them; the slips clung on to impossible catches. I hit four fours off successive balls on Mitcham Green; I ran two men (of my own side) out in a match against Barclays Bank. I had a chequered and not unusually successful season; but I felt welded into a community of cricketers as rarely before in my life.

It is difficult to diagnose the reason for Bob's alchemical power over the team. It waxes and wanes, of course, but it is still there, and it controls the young and the old alike. (Unhappily for the second eleven, he has lately been translated in a crisis to captain the first.) Passively, with no authoritarian nonsense, with sometimes less inspiration and sometimes more, he exists to combine all our tantalizing virtues into a workable whole, and he does it. Not entirely by taking thought, either; it is a matter of instinctive personality. In his eager terrier-like youth, when he fidgeted himself to the verge of I daren't say how many nervous crises, we laughed at him and patted his head; in his eager early middle-age when his hair has gone grey and his face has withdrawn into pits and hollows and wrinkles, he has stopped fidgeting altogether and his quivering nervousness has been miraculously replaced by a curious serenity that communicates itself to the whole team. Yet it does not seem the passiveness of age, for he bowls quick medium still and can at a pinch be relied on for sixty runs that will change a game round. Save for Len and Jerry he is still the best bat in the club. There is still in his face the superb single-mindedness of youth; he is the boy eternal whom I embodied earlier, though he makes an immense parade of senility. "You know, Ron," he says to me often, his youthful simplicity blending queerly with his heavy air of unfathomable experience, so that I have the uneasy feeling that I am being given a fatherly talking-to by my own son, "You know, Ron, we can't go on like this for ever. We've got to give the younger boys a chance." And he succeeds in looking inscrutably wizened for about a quarter of a minute, and then takes 3 for 7 in five overs, catches the opening batsman one-handed at short-leg and makes 42 not out to win the match by two wickets five minutes from time. In the intervals of cricket he goes in unsuccessfully for fishing and, equally unsuccessfully, for trying to wean me from Socialism, a condition which most of the other members of the team have accepted with resignation after a great deal of frenetic argument, but not Bob, who affects the most bewildered puzzlement at the very notion that anybody in or out of his senses could dream for a single moment of being a Socialist. One of these arguments, which I always find exceptionally stimulating, occurred at the end of last season when, on the way home from the final autumnal match, the team stopped off at a hotel in Kingston and engaged in a chicken dinner of magnificent proportions. Towards the end a terrific political argument blew up, I as usual speaking for one side and the others for the other. I do not say that tempers were strained; they were not, but voices were raised, and probably a glass or two was knocked over. It died away as soon as it had risen, and left us all where we were before; a little over-heated perhaps but still friendly. "Never mind, Ronnie," said the equable Maurice Gates. "It's no good arguing with Bob, especially as he's a better Socialist than you are yourself."

Maurice and Douglas Gates, veteran brothers whose ages add up to a hundred or more on paper but who look in the field about thirty each, form the really experienced core of the side that Bob Ward leads. Long-headed civil servants both, they reveal obverse sides of the same family coin, Douglas being mercurial, breathless, voluble, versatile, multitudinously adept,* and Maurice steady, canny, sardonic, resourceful, restful. Douglas has a son, Martin,

---

* It is solemnly recorded of this excellent cricketer that on one occasion he was rendered so eager and purposeful by the stresses of a moment of intense crisis that he arrived briskly at the wicket without his bat.

who combines his own ability of eye and wrist with Maurice's unshakable phlegm, and is to my mind the most likely successor to the Smith-Cole-Bush tradition that the club at present harbours. Together with the square defiant wicket-keeper Ted Gray who can hit screaming sixes over the bowler's head with a wide scything action, and Tag Taylor, the keenest club cricketer in England, with whom I have interminable political arguments, these form the Old Guard, if you take in as well the pale and elongated figure of my good friend Reg Flavell, my opening partner and unspeakably harassed team secretary. If neither he nor I got out we should make ideal partners, he watchful with a fine defence and no scoring strokes, I as brilliant as flowers in May with about as much stability as Eno's Fruit Salts. "I can't do a thing, boy," says Reg to me after playing a maiden over or so. "Go on, you get 'em as quick as you can." And if I don't get caught, I do what I can; and on the whole it makes out. Reg specializes in fatuous telephone conversations and has accepted my fixation on poetry; so that once while he and I, not out batsmen during a shower, were strolling somewhere in seclusion with our pads on, he solemnly recited for me from memory *The Old Ships* by James Elroy Flecker, which he had learned long since and lost awhile; and on the occasion when the club had had a new issue of caps and we were all wearing the brand-new horrors, he stopped me and whispered hoarsely on his way to cover-point between overs:

> "*Of all the boys in their new caps,*
> *Is Ron the best? Perhaps,*"

and retired sniggering to his place. Whereat, I, cudgelling my brains through an over or so in the slips, met him front to front as we crossed over once more and hissed balefully in his unsuspecting ears:

> "*It may not be so bad in hell*
> *If heaven should contain Flavell,*"

and was delighted to see him giggle so uncontrollably that he let the next ball through his legs for four.

There they are, the men of Banstead, no better in the bulk and no worse, and certainly no more distinctive, than any eight or nine club sides that they may meet from weekend to weekend. Ashtead, Cheam, Epsom; Barclays Bank, Beddington, Old Whitgiftians; Cyphers, East Molesey, Spencer—any and all of these may provide material as rich for a lifetime's companionship at this most companionable of games. I only write of the men of Banstead because they, like the village they represent, are an essential part of my experience, like the men of Surrey I have already tried to honour, who are blessed with a more illustrious but certainly no more picturesque ground to play out their patterns on. Above all it is the ground on which we are so lucky to play that returns to my thoughts as often as, even oftener than, the men who use it; for there are great companies of them, and they come and they change and they go, but there is only one Banstead cricket green and that remains. George Muggeridge could not renew his green leaves like the limes; Len Cole, once he has cast his flambeaux like the chestnut, cannot resume them next spring. So it is against the setting of this ground that I see the moments which bind me to the reality of the past—the stupendous hit by Geoff Harrison of the Old Whitgiftians, which seemed to mount twice the height of the limes and which Teddy Minnion caught above his head with his heels on the cinder path; Bill Smith's raking straight drive, an impossible catch by Len Cole at close short-leg off a full-powered hook, the six I remember, if no one else does, because it was the very last ball of the season and I hit it over the lime trees into the tennis courts. The seasons pass, and the club's faces change, except of course the secretary's, owlish and reliable and humorous, the same today as twenty years ago and for all I know twenty years before that, and in twenty years' time, who will lie down beside Stanley Baker to be rolled into the pitch if the necessity should come, and believe me it will test the roller.

The seasons pass, we can do nothing about it, simply play Saturday by Saturday, home and away, acting out these simple but elaborate manœuvres as if our lives depended on it. For a season or two we remain static, the same team foregathers, plays, drinks and disperses, and one Saturday and one season becomes indistinguishable from another. For a season or two Reg and I, I hope, will leave the pavilion after tea (Bob's eccentric habit with the choice of innings, inherited by his successes, has permanently ruined my appreciation of the refreshment break) with the taste of cake in our mouths, to face our opponents' total and our opponents' fast bowlers. For a season or two we will go expertly through the motions perfected for our imitation by the great—touching our caps, taking guard, looking round the field, taking a firmer grip on the bat handle, flexing our legs, and composing ourselves in readiness to receive the bowling. Up to that point we are apt pupils enough; it is only from then on that our competence begins to crack.

> Et ce n'est point du tout la prendre pour modèle,
> Ma sœur, que de tousser et de cracher comme elle.

We can cough and spit like Hutton and Compton; we can only bat like Flavell and Mason. But after all we are Banstead 2nd XI and not England; and we each have our parcels of small triumph before age overtakes us. In Banstead I have seen in little the same dark transformations that I have marked in the larger cosmos of the first-class game; they are no doubt occurring as inevitably in me as in the others whom I have seen age and wither in my twenty years' acquaintance. Yet on the field or at the lighted bar or in the dressing-room or about the green as it darkens under the evening shades of the lime and the chestnut, we carry on the continuity with relish. " He enjoys his cricket," said one member to me of a younger player, a headstrong likeable colt with unbridled energy and dash. " True," I replied, " true enough. And the rest of us? We simply detest it, I suppose? "

CHAPTER TEN

THE RITUAL AND THE REALITY

I SET out at the beginning of this book to find something that has puzzled me all my life—the secret of the urgent fascination of this game. I have loved it for thirty years and more and season after season I go to it with ardour unabated. It does not matter to me very much whether I am playing or watching, though after a day at Lord's I feel I ought to have been playing, and make jerky embryonic gestures illustrative of ideal strokes as I walk down to Baker Street Station; on the whole I can enjoy playing with a completeness of response which is denied me while watching, though my satisfaction is more often than not bitterly tempered by a realization of how much more pleasant it would be if I could have been really good at it. The beatitude of the masters of the game, who know the quality of their own skill and can savour it expertly, must be rich indeed. It is for those of us who know enough and feel enough about its emotional and æsthetic range, without having the ability to realize it in action more than once or twice in our lives, to suffer the torments of Tantalus nearly every time we play. Victor Buckingham tells me of a friend of his own, well known in his own way in club cricket, who has for years and years played regularly twice a week with the utmost willingness and application, who is exceptionally keen and knowledgeable with a vast fund of interest in and knowledge of the ultimate recesses and finer points, and yet who is cursed by fortune with an absence of proficiency that is not merely negative but heartbreakingly positive. At the wicket, with the ball, in the field, he could not blunder more if he were one's arthritic grandmother; his high enthusiasm adds, pitifully, to his weekly discomfiture rather than dilutes it. Yet there is no readier helper in the club, no nicer colleague or friendlier appraiser of the game's merits. " If he has his proper reward," says Victor, " he will go in first with Jack Hobbs in Heaven." Very nice, but here below what reward does he get? Precious small; yet the game enslaves him. (Incidentally, this Elysian business will cause celestial heartburnings, for it is a match in which we have all booked ourselves places. I am due to go in Number 3, presumably after Victor's friend has hit a sparkling hundred, or more likely, knowing him, run himself blunderingly out before he has had a ball; and after Hobbs has got out, passing me on his way to the pavilion and saying " Well, it's up to you boys now," Hammond and I are to put on over 200. I do not know how this clashes with other people's plans; but I assure you that so far as I am concerned that is what has been arranged.)

We can agree about the fascination, then, but it is a problem to explain it. As I said, I set out to do it; but I find I have not; I have only in a random and reckless way described it. And I can describe something over and over again, with a repetition here and a shift of emphasis there, until the thing itself is as clear as daylight or as clear as mud, and I will still be no nearer an explanation. I have been driven to the conclusion that it is useless to try. Those who have been bitten will understand before starting to read; those who have not will never understand at all, however hard they or I may try. And the world seems, or seemed last summer, almost completely and clearly divided into those who have been bitten and those who have not. There is no third party. The addicts need not be converted, the unconverted are unconvertible. Therefore, I repeat, an explanation is unnecessary, as the initiates do not call for it and the others would not listen.

To explain it to one's worrying self, though, that is the question. That is at bottom the purpose of writing all this at all; there have naturally been attendant pleasures which I have not shrunk from indulging as I went along, as quips at the expense of my fellows or nostalgia for the illicit gratification of myself, but these were incidentals and it would all have happened without them. I wrote it to explain my obsession to myself; and yet I did not explain it at all, I merely described, somewhat lengthily, its chief manifestations. What was the good of that?

Yet, the timely thought strikes me, if we take what is I hope not too impudent an analogy, being wide awake and conscious of the seeming absurdity but also of a certain relative value which may help us, if a man is distressed or puzzled being in love, has he ever clarified his dilemmas or his bewilderments by seeking to explain scientifically what love is? Many have tried, but I would still like to know one who has succeeded. All that has been done by even the rarest of imaginations so beset is to render a series of dramatic impressions of the state of love, from the viewpoint of one mood or another, and we are accordingly enriched by the lyrics of Catullus, or the sonnets of Shakespeare or Ronsard, or the songs of Robert Burns; or *Madame Bovary* or *The Ordeal of Richard Feverel* or *Antony and Cleopatra* or *Le Grand Meaulnes* or *The Rainbow*. And now if we can come a very long way downstairs indeed, what have I done myself with the similar problem of this game but render as best I can a series of more or less dramatic impressions of its impact upon me or upon my life? Is this perhaps after all the best way to go about my quest?

Maybe Marcel Proust would have helped. He of all great writers came nearest to the satisfactory anatomization of the elusive principles which it was his life and his death to pursue; and in my search through cricket literature for any light on my bewilderment I have been driven at times to wish that some vast switch of unpredictable and unimaginable fortune had visited him with an obsession for the game. What elaborate and kaleidoscopic conjecturings we should have been treated to, what deftly and poignantly manipulated emotions would have started up at the sound of bat meeting ball! It will have been clear from much that I have already said that certain observations of Proust's on the decaying forces inherent in the passage of Time have been of great value to me when I have been considering the place of this game in the uneventful story of my own life. But how much more if he could have provided the actuality rather than the analogy—if he had played regularly in the holidays for the Combray eleven, taken a team down (with Saint Loup in it for certain) to play Balbec, bored the Duchesse de Guermantes, not to mention Albertine, with his conversations on the game, and made frantic half-snobbish overtures to the Baron de Charlus or to Swann (who would no doubt have been members) to get himself put up for the M.C.C. . . . but here the imagination, already overstrained, veers clean off the rails and out of sight. I

quieten myself with a reminiscence of the photograph of Marcel
at the tennis party, a grotesque affair in which, although I confess he
looks happy enough, he is the reverse of congruous. No, with
reluctance we must face the impossible. He could never have done
it; but what a wonderful opportunity the Fates (or was it the
Graces?) missed!

The literature of cricket fails us; we draw a blank every time.
John Nyren reveals a delightful humanity and in the celebrated
passage about the ale unlocks the door on a poignant sense of
deprivation. Nearly a hundred years after him Francis Thompson's
uneven lyric captured for a breathlessly short moment a hint of the
uncapturable mystery—with him it is the lost mystery that haunts,
his field of shades, his ghostly white figures in a dim sea of memory,
his soundless-clapping host, his own drowning tears, all knelled
home to the heart by those three dreadful syllables " Long ago."
Because his poem is answered, in little, in all of us, it is treasured
as the one indisputably " great " piece of literature that the game
has ever inspired or attracted. Yet what does it do? Perpetrates
a self-pitying emotionalism, and so, in his own yeoman way,
does Nyren. And I cannot think of any latter-day master, Cardus
or Arlott, Robertson-Glasgow or Blunden, who can do anything
more. Perhaps the would-be anatomizers are better advised to give
it up; they are bending to themselves a joy.

I too have done the same. I began by establishing the formal ritual
on which every complex and preordained manœuvre of the match
is founded; I tried to show how a romantic colour has been overlaid
on to the bare movements, and my first chapter was an attempt to
show how fertile a field is the cricket field for æsthetic appreciation,
upon which emotion, both genuine and spurious, can play and
build. Then I adventured into the personal obsession, gave examples
with as much humiliating detail as I could recall of the way in
which this ritual and this romance were given flesh and blood
in my own experience—my own flesh and blood as well as the
flesh and blood of the public heroes I followed. My own adventures
in the game, as spectator and as player, modest enough though
they have been, have been the only authentic channel along which
I could usefully approach the heart of the matter, and after all,
what have they brought me, save this joy that cannot get itself

into words when I try to find a reason for it? Well, there may be one thing that experience has proved to me: that the ritual and the romance are not of any value without a strong leavening of human character. Reading our papers and our *Wisdens* we sometimes forget that here is a game played out by individuals, by twenty-two little worlds all vitally differentiated, and not by units expressible by white figures on a scoreboard. Otherwise we might as well leave it to the roulette wheel, as Victor and I did long ago. But if you have read as far as this you will have understood by now what part individuals and their characteristic idiosyncrasies have played in the development of my appreciation of cricket; how in their several ways R. E. S. Wyatt, and Victor Buckingham, and Major Luther, and the Surrey eleven of the twenties, and Jack Hobbs, and Walter Hammond, and Denis Compton, and Bill Smith, and Len Cole all added the intense importance of individuality not only to the way in which they approached and fulfilled their parts in the game but (unwittingly) to the way in which they presented the game of cricket, as a vivid personal experience, to me.

And even so it would be a mistake, as a general rule, to regard the game as plumbing the deepest springs of human character. It is a mistake that is made fairly widely. The character that Len Cole or Len Hutton may bring to the art and practice of their cricket may be a fraction only, and possibly not a very important fraction, of their composite and elaborate personalities. I must make it clear that at all times during this book I have been talking of these men, some of whom I have met but most of whom I have not, as cricketers only. That this may mislead *sub specie æternitatis* may be lightly illustrated by the example of one of the most capable and clearheaded public servants I know, who for many years captained the departmental side I assisted and still assist, and who was in his day a very nasty opening bowler indeed. Endowed in his official person with a mental precision and authority to astonish the world, this admirable fellow put off on the cricket field his professional incisiveness, which made him an endearing but vague captain and a companion of attractive aimlessness. It was related of him that one afternoon two successive catches towered high in the air over circling knots of fieldsmen, and that on the first occasion he cried in a commanding voice "Catch it!" and on the second in an equally commanding voice " One of you! " That both were dropped goes without saying. He it was who bowled Willie Watson first ball without knowing who he was; he it was too who, on the successful conclusion of an inter-departmental final, received the coveted shield from the official dignitary making the presentation, blushed red and speechless and dropped the trophy on the floor, splitting it from top to bottom. Or did he? And was it true in fact, or only in essence? Or does it matter anyway, so amiable was the cricket when he was in command? One remark anyway is absolutely authentic. On one nightmare occasion when his side were dismissed for 27 by about a quarter past three and their opponents had the rest of the afternoon to employ over this not very formidable task, this captain on leading his team into the field sniffed the air, looked hungrily about, and said " Well! We've got them on the board. They've got all their work cut out now."

Diversity of character and diversity of humour are essential ingredients without which the ritualistic movement, expert though it may be, would provide a tasteless dish indeed. And we are driven once more to acknowledge the game's close analogy with the full life, in that its elements of conflict, often long sustained, its elements of irony and farce, its corresponding elements of what may by courtesy be called tragedy, combine with its potentially illimitable resources of æsthetic beauty and grace to present to the responsive mind what is more than a spectacle and more than an exercise, but a kind of emotional experience. Now I am not going to be mistaken here; I would refer you back to the phrase " close analogy." I do not claim for cricket the authenticity of conflict, force, beauty, tragedy, or what you will; I merely claim for it a complex activity which in its own context can provide similar sensations in the mind. The acting of an emotional situation on a stage can, as we well know, surprise with relief or dismay and purge with pity and terror. Participation in a game, especially in a game compact of artistry and beauty, can summon in the most unemotional consciousness the simulacra of kindred excitements. There is nothing artificial about it if we are careful not to attribute to it moral and imaginative qualities to which it makes no pretence; and there is nothing artificial about the friendships that go with it and the happy relationships which it promotes. Its comedy is endearing and its tragedy is for the most part without sting. (I say this with deference to my Banstead friend, a moderate batsman, who cherishes a grudge against Fate because the highest innings he ever played, an innings he would give his ears to play again in delicious memory, is a completely closed book to him; since, going for a quick run at the very start, he knocked himself unconscious on the handle of his bat, and though he recovered sufficiently to continue, he cannot remember a single moment or incident of the brilliant and uncharacteristic fifty he was told he proceeded to make.)

The fascination is still there and the fascination is unexplained; we cannot bend to ourselves its peculiar joy. The secret is, I suppose, the secret that I knew all the time I should have to face; that we must kiss the joy as it flies. No one by taking thought can add a cubit to his stature; no one by refining his intellectual doubts into platitudes of unhelpful generality can proceed an inch nearer to the core of his problems. Not, at any rate, with something so elusive as this. Say, then, that it is a man-made activity of a strenuous combative nature, designed and leading to no end but enjoyment. That will have to stand; to elaborate on that I would need to write a further dissertation upon enjoyment, which since the Puritan Revolution and the era of the Nonconformist conscience has been a philosophical idea upon which the English have frowned, as it is deeply ingrained in their consciousness that if they are really enjoying themselves they are committing an obscure but definite sin, always provided that they are absolved from this dark responsibility if there is money at the end of it.

I have enjoyed my cricket; and am salving my own Nonconformist conscience in a superfluous effort to find out why. The conclusion I came to is this, that to find the secret I must kiss the joy as it flies and I will not need to go irritably searching about after reasons. Keats saw this in his own context long since and counselled passivity as the absolute essential for a right appreciation of experience. Next season I will therefore take the game as it comes, intensifying my concentration upon the moment and making no further philosophical demands upon the thin air. It is a game which demands and deserves the undivided mind, always providing that in your concentration you omit not the humaner aspects of the pastime. To kiss the joy as it flies I must watch the bowler even more keenly as I crouch at first slip in the looming green shadow of the chestnuts and the limes; I must say over and over again to myself as I look round the field before receiving my first ball and grinning at Reg at the other end, " Don't slash at the rising ball on the off in the first over, don't slash at the rising ball on the off in the first over." And the same when I crane at the Oval or lounge more comfortably at Lord's, marking equably and with renewed pleasure the appearance of my old familiar friends who do not know me—I must accept their activity and analyse its *raison d'être* no more. It is enough that it is a good game.